Savita
pp 20, 22, 25
p 71 nearabout
72 "

DIMENSIONS BEYOND THE KNOWN

OSHO

Translation from the original Hindi
by Sadhu Anand Chit

Editing by Ma Ananda Prem,
Swami Krishna Prabhu
Typesetting by Ma Prem Arya
Design by Ma Krishna Gopa
Photography by Swami Veet Pramad
Paintings by Swami Shivananda
Production by Swami Prem Visarjan,
Ma Punyo
Printing by Mohndruck, Gütersloh,
West Germany

Published by
The Rebel Publishing House GmbH
 Venloer Straße 5 - 7
 5000 Cologne
 West Germany

 1075 N.W. Murray Road
 Suite 258
 Portland, OR 97229
 USA

Copyright Neo-Sannyas International
Second Edition
All rights reserved

No part of this book may be reproduced
or transmitted in any form or by any
means electronic or mechanical
including photocopying or recording or
by any information storage and retrieval
system without permission in writing
from the publisher.

ISBN 3-89338-061-2

CONTENTS

1. Nothing Else to Tell Except This   1

2. Why I Have Come   39

3. Paths are Many, the Travelers are Few   77

4. This is a Time of Crisis   115

5. The Birth of a New Man   141

6. Life is Full of Mysteries   159

INTRODUCTION

OSHO is without doubt the most controversial figure this century has produced. He is an enlightened master who has been hounded from the world stage by most of the "free" national governments only to rise again in the manner of the proverbial phoenix. How does one silence truth?

In this book, which contains six talks given in Bombay between 1970 and 1973, Osho gives the reader a new perspective on the universe and its infinite possibilities. He takes the esoteric and with His incredible lucidity transforms it into the exoteric, the known.

This is the only book of His I have read where He speaks of His past in such terms. He describes time and its relevance to both His former life and the events of His current life. He describes the process of death, the Tibetan Bardo, and rebirth, not in the usual terms of intellectual speculation and hypothesis but in terms of His own personal experience, of one who knows.

That Osho is able to take such metaphysical concepts and explain them in such a simple yet comprehensive way is one of His many mysteries.

He is, like the subjects He discusses in this volume, as mysterious as existence itself.

Swami Anand Yogendra, B.A., Ll.B.
Poona, December 1989

1

NOTHING ELSE TO TELL EXCEPT THIS

February 28, 1970

I have read Your literature;
I have heard You.
Your language has hypnotic charm and is very clear.
Sometimes You speak on Mahavira,
sometimes on Krishna or Buddha
and sometimes You tell about Jesus
and Mohammed as well. You divulge the secrets
of the Gita in a most inspiring manner,
You give discourses on the Upanishads and the Vedas,
and You would not hesitate to go to temples
or churches to give discourses.
All the same, You maintain that You are not influenced
by any of the personages mentioned above.
You say that You have nothing to do with them
and You do not agree with them.
Continuously, You criticize and shatter
to pieces the ancient religious beliefs and scriptures.
What is Your purpose?
Do You want to establish Your own religion?
Do You want to show that You have limitless knowledge?
Or do You want to confuse everyone?
You speak and explain in words,

but at the same time You say that "You will not reach anywhere by clinging to words." You say, "Neither believe me nor cling to me; otherwise you will commit the same mistake." You also say that this negation itself is an invitation. Kindly explain who and what You are and what You want to do and say. What is Your intention?

FIRSTLY, I am not influenced by Mahavira, Buddha, Christ or Mohammed. It is the beauty of religion that in one sense it is always old. It is in this sense that religious experiences are known to many persons. No religious experience is such that one can say that "It is mine only."

There are two reasons for this. Firstly, on having a religious experience, the sense of "my-ness" dies. That is why, in this world, a claim of "my-ness" can be made for everything, but not for religious experience. This is the only experience which falls beyond the orbit of "my-ness," because this experience can be had only on the death of "my-ness." That is why the claim of "my-ness" could be there for everything, but not for a religious experience. Nor can anyone say that such an experience is new, because truth is neither new nor old.

It is in this sense that I speak of Mahavira, Jesus, Krishna, Christ and others: they had religious experiences. When I say that I am not influenced by them, I only mean that what I say comes out of my own experience and knowledge. I speak about them, I use their names, because what I have known tallies with what they have known. But for me the test is my own experience.

On that test I find them right, and that is why I use their names. I am telling what I tell out of my own experience. They also prove right in my experience; therefore, I talk about them. They are my witnesses; they are witnesses of my experience as well. But this experience cannot be called new. Yet, in another sense, it can be called new. This is the riddle and fundamental mystery of religion.

A religious experience can be called new because to whomsoever this experience dawns it is absolutely new and happening for the first time. It has not occurred before. It may have occurred to someone else, but for the one who has experienced it for the first time it is new. It is so new to him that he cannot conceive that such an experience could have occurred to someone else.

As long as this experience has a relationship with the consciousness of the person, the experience is for the first time. The experience is so novel, so fresh, that whosoever experiences it never feels that it can ever be old. It is like the freshness of a flower opening in the morning, its petals wet with dew, the early rays of the sun falling on them. Looking at this flower, one who may have seen it for the first time cannot say that this flower is old, even though every morning a new flower opens.

Every morning the dew and the rays of the sun fall on new flowers. Someone's eyes may have seen these flowers daily, but whoever has seen the flower for the first time in this setting cannot even think that this flower could have been seen before. It is so new that if he says that truth can never be old, that it is always new and original, he is not wrong.

We say that religion is ancient and eternal because truth is everlasting. But religion is also new, because whenever truth is realized the experience is new, fresh, virginal. If a person believes that religion is old or if he believes that religion is new, he will not be inconsistent with truth. If he says that truth is eternal and maintains that it cannot be new, you will not find him to be inconsistent. Another person, on the other hand, may hold that truth is always new.

Gurdjieff, if asked, would say that religion is eternal and ancient; Krishnamurti, if asked, would say that it is absolutely new, that it can never be old. But both of them are consistent.

The question that you ask me could not be asked either to Gurdjieff or Krishnamurti. Their answers would only be half-truths.

Half-truths can always be consistent, but a total truth is always inconsistent because in a total truth the opposite is also included.

One person may say that light and only light is the truth. He will then ignore darkness and look upon it as false. But just by calling darkness false, the existence of darkness is not denied. He can be consistent because he denies darkness and does not bother about its existence. His philosophy can be clear, straight and consistent like mathematics. In his philosophy there will be no riddles. However, someone else who says that there is darkness and only darkness everywhere, that light is only an illusion, can also be consistent.

Difficulty arises with a person who says that there is darkness and there is light also. The person who accepts the existence of both accepts the fact that darkness and light are only two extremes of the same thing. If darkness and light are two different things, then by the increase of light darkness should not be reduced, and by the decrease of light darkness should not increase. But it is a fact that by the increase or decrease of light, darkness can be decreased or increased. The meaning is clear: that light is somewhere a part of darkness and vice versa. Both are two ends of one thing.

Therefore, when I try to tell the *whole* truth, the difficulty is that I seem inconsistent. I am telling at the same time two things that seem contradictory. I say that truth is eternal and it is wrong to call it new; at the same time I also say that truth is always new and there is no sense in calling it old. When I say both of these things together, I am attempting to catch the whole truth at once in its complete fullness.

Whenever truth is told in its fullness, in its multiple meanings, then opposing, inconsistent statements will have to be made. Mahavira's theory of *syatavada* is only an attempt at balancing the opposing views. Against whatever is said in the first sentence an opposite statement will have to be made in the second sentence. In this way, the opposite, which would otherwise remain unsaid, is also included and comprehended.

If the opposite is left out, the truth will remain incomplete.

Therefore, all truths that appear clear and unambiguous are really half-truths. Inconsistency is inherent in truth, and that is its beauty and its complexity. But its power lies in the inclusion of polar opposites.

It is interesting to note that something false cannot include its opposite. That which is false can live only at the opposite pole of a truth, while truth absorbs within itself its own opposite. That is why falsity is not very ambiguous; it is clear.

Life as a whole is founded on polar opposites. In life there is nothing that occurs without the struggle of opposites, but we try with our minds and our reasoning to eliminate the inconsistencies. Our reasoning is an attempt to become consistent while the total will appear inconsistent. In existence, all inconsistencies are there together. Death and life are bound together.

Logic appears neat because it divides things into opposites. For logic, life is life and death is death; both cannot go together. In logic we say that A is A, and it is not B. We say life is life; it is not death. Similarly, death is death; it is not life. In this way we make our concepts neat and mathematical, but the mystery of life is lost. That is why you cannot arrive at truth by reasoning. One is an attempt to be consistent, and the other, by its very nature, is inconsistent. You can, therefore, achieve consistency by reasoning. You can reason so well, so logically, that you cannot be defeated in argument. But you will miss truth.

I am not a philosopher or a logician, but I always use logic. I am using this only for the purpose of leading your thinking to the point where you can be pushed out of it. If reasoning is not exhausted, one cannot go beyond it. I am climbing on a ladder, but this ladder is not my goal; it has to be given up. I use reasoning only to know what is beyond it. I do not want to establish anything by reasoning. What I want instead is to prove its uselessness.

My statements will, therefore, be inconsistent and illogical. As long as they appear to be logical, please understand that I am only using a system that makes them appear so. I am preparing the groundwork for what is to follow. I am tuning up the instruments; the music has not yet started.

Where the line of demarcation between reason and non-reason is lost is where my original, my unique music begins. As soon as the instruments are attuned, the music will start. But do not misunderstand the tuning for the music; otherwise it will create difficulties. You will ask, "What is the matter? Before you were using a hammer for the drum. Why are you no longer using it?" But a hammer is only for tuning the drum, not for playing it. Once the drum is tuned, the hammer is of no use. A drum cannot be played with a hammer.

In the same way, reasoning is only a preparation for what is beyond reasoning. One of the difficulties I have is that those who approve of my reasoning will find after a few moments that I am taking them into an area of darkness. As long as one can see reasoning, there is light and things look bright and clear. But then someone will say that I promised to show him the light and now I am talking about leading him into darkness. He will, therefore, be displeased with me and will tell me, "I like what you have said until now, but I can go no further with you." He trusted me to reason out the truth for him, and then I tell him that he must go beyond reasoning in order to reach it.

Those who believe in trust will also not accept me, not follow me, not walk with me, because they want me to talk only about incomprehensible mysteries. Thus, both types of individuals will have problems with me. Believers in reason will only follow me up to a certain point, while those who believe in trust, who believe in the irrational, will not follow me at all, never understanding that only if they follow past a certain point can I take them into thoughtlessness.

I understand this. Life is like that. Reason can only be an instrument, not the goal. I will, therefore, always make illogical statements after talking about fully logical matters. These statements will appear inconsistent, but they have been well thought out and are not made without a reason. There is a clear reason from my side.

I will say at certain times that I am not influenced by Mahavira, Buddha, Krishna or Christ, that I do not say anything under their influence, that everything I say, I say only after knowing it myself. Nevertheless, when I came to my own realization, I knew that it was identical to that which had been attained by these others before me. Thus, when I am speaking about them or quoting what they have said, I myself forget that I have been speaking about them. I merge with them so totally that their statements become my own.

In fact, I do not see any difference between my statements and theirs. When I start to speak about them there is the deep realization that I am only speaking about me. Therefore, when I repeat their statements, I make no conditions. I dissolve myself completely in them and in their words. Those who have heard me say that I am not influenced by these others will wonder, "How is it that you become one with them? Even those who are under their complete influence do not do so; they maintain a distance."

Those who are influenced by someone or something will, of necessity, have to maintain a certain distance between themselves and the source of the influence. Those who are influenced are ignorant. We are influenced only in ignorance. With self-knowledge the very word 'influence' has no meaning.

In self-knowledge there is no question of influence. Rather, there is a similarity of experience, a similar resonance, the hearing of similar voices. If I am singing and the same tune is coming at the same time from someone else, my rhythm and the rhythm of the other singer are so at one with each other that there is no room between us for being influenced. In order to be influenced, in order to be a disciple, distance is necessary, the other is necessary.

However, as far as I am concerned there is no distance. When I start explaining a statement of Mahavira or when I speak on the Gita of Krishna, I am only more or less explaining my own statements. Krishna or Christ or Mahavira provide an opportunity, an excuse, an occasion to speak, but I soon forget that I was speaking about them. I start with them, but end only on what I have known. I am not even aware of when I cease talking about them and begin to explain my own statements, of when I have merged totally with them.

Perhaps it would interest you to know that I have not read the Gita even once. I have started to read it often, but upon reading eight or ten lines I felt that it was enough and closed the book. When I speak on the Gita, I am really hearing it for the first time as I speak about it. As I have no background in it, I have no way of criticizing it. One who has studied the Gita, who has pondered over and thought deeply about its statements, can only criticize or define what he has read. Not having read the Gita, I can do neither.

Another interesting thing to mention is that when I pick up the Gita to read I put it back after a few moments, but when I come across some very ordinary book I read it through from beginning to end because it is not a part of my experience. This may seem odd to you. I cannot restrain myself from reading through an ordinary book, because it is not within the range of my experience. Yet, when I begin to read the Gita, I put the book back after reading only a few lines of it, since I do not feel that it will open up anything new to me.

If a spy story is given to me, I may go through it fully, because for me it may be something new. But Krishna's Gita seems as if it was written by me. I know it, because whatever is written in it is known to me. Without reading it is known.

Therefore, when I speak on the Gita, I do not actually speak on the Gita; it is only an excuse. I start with the Gita, but I speak only about what I want to speak and only about that which I can speak. If you feel that I have dwelt a great deal on the Gita, it is not because I am influenced by Krishna, but because Krishna said the very same things that I am saying.

Thus, what I am doing is not a commentary on the Gita. What Tilak has said on the Gita, what Gandhi has said on the Gita, was their commentary or explanation of the Gita. They were under the deep influence of the Gita. But what I am saying does not come from the Gita at all. The tunes that are touched upon by the Gita are touched within me as well. They lead me to my own tunes; I begin to explain my own self. The Gita only provides me with an occasion. When I am speaking on Krishna, during those very moments that I am most deeply revealing Krishna you will begin to feel that I am talking about my own self. It is in those moments that I am speaking only about me.

The same thing is true with Mahavira, Christ, Lao Tzu or Mohammed. For me, what differentiates one of them from another is only a difference in name. They are different lamps, but the light that shines within them is the same. Whether that light is burning in the lamp of Mohammed or in the lamp of Mahavira or of Buddha does not make any difference to me.

Many times I will speak against Mohammed or Mahavira or Buddha. This creates a problem. I am speaking deeply about them, and yet, at the same time, I am speaking against them as well. Whenever I seem to be speaking against them, it appears to be so only because the listener is giving importance to the lamp. But for me, when I am revealing something very deep, the emphasis is on the light. So whenever I appear to be speaking against, it is because the emphasis is on the lamp and not the light.

When I see a person enamored of the lamp, of the material with which it is made, I will always speak against the lamp. The person will be confused. It is natural that he will be confused, because for him there is no distinction between Mahavira the lamp and Mahavira the eternal light. For him, the lamp and the light are the same. That is why, when it appears to me that someone is placing too much emphasis on the lamp, I start speaking against it. When I feel that it is light that is discussed, I become one with it. This is the difference.

There is a difference between the lamp of Mahavira and the lamp of Mohammed. It is only due to this difference that there is a difference between a Jaina and a Mohammedan. Lamps are made differently. The lamp of Christ and the lamp of Buddha are also different; they are bound to be so. But these are differences of body, of surroundings and of shape.

To those who are fond of shapes and surroundings, that light will not be visible, because whosoever sees the light will forget the lamp. It is impossible that one will still remember the lamp after he has seen the light. The lamp is remembered only after the light is no longer seen.

The condition of a follower is such that he can only remain in the dark shadow of the lamp and look out from there. From there he cannot see the light; only the bottom of the lamp is seen. The bottoms of all lamps are different, and there is deep darkness under them. Their followers stand quarreling over the bottoms. Therefore, whenever I see someone standing in someone's shadow, I speak against this rather harshly.

That is why I always say that a follower can never understand. To become a follower, he has to stand in the shadow, in the darkness, beneath the lamp. The more one is a follower, the more he is in the density of the shadow. Followers who are standing on the shadow's periphery can understand others a little, but those who are directly in the shadow's density can never understand. However, if someone really wants to see the light, he will have to go completely out of the shadow's periphery. Once he sees the light, the controversy over lamps no longer has any meaning for him.

Thus, for me, there is no difference whether I speak on Christ or Krishna or Buddha. I am talking about the same light – a light which has illuminated many lamps. But I am not influenced by the lamps. I am speaking only about that which I know. Whenever I feel a certain resonance, whenever I feel that the same note is vibrating, I am not able to deny it, because to deny it would be equally wrong. It would be like standing with my back to the light. The follower commits the error of sitting under the bottom of the lamp. Turning one's back or sitting in the shadow are both similar errors. But if you ask Krishnamurti, he will not accept this resonance. He will not accept that whatever has happened to him could also have happened to Krishna. He will not accept that what has happened to him could have happened to others as well. He will not discuss this.

This is wrong because truth is totally impersonal. The greatness of truth does not diminish if one accepts that it was also revealed to someone else. On the contrary, its greatness is enhanced; it does not diminish. Truth is not so weak that it becomes stale simply because it has also been experienced by someone else. Therefore, the temptation to deny that truth could be shared is also wrong.

My difficulty, therefore, is this: that *wherever* I see truth, I will accept it. I am not influenced at all. But wherever I see that in the name of truth people are changing to something that is not truth I shall deny it and oppose it. Whatever I do, I do totally. That is why I become difficult to understand. I am against compromises because by compromise nobody can ever reach truth.

It is my nature to say whatever I say with the full force of my vital being. So if someone is talking about the light, I will say that Mahavira is God, Krishna is an incarnation of God and Jesus is the son of God. But if someone who is only talking about the lamps says these things, then I say that the speaker is guilty of a criminal act. In both these cases, whatever I assert, whenever I assert it, I shall stand fully for what I have said.

When I am making a statement about something, I do not ever remember my previous statements on the subject. But the statements are true and complete and do not negate each other. If I am speaking about your body my statement will be death-oriented, but if I am talking about you I will say that you are immortal. Do not think that these two statements are in opposition, however; they do not negate each other. There is no necessity for any compromise between them. Your body is bound to die; it is death-oriented.

If you believe that you are the body, then I will state with full force that you will die. I will not allow even for a slight chance of your being saved. If the discussion is about the soul, then I will say that you have never been born at all. Then you are unborn and immortal; the question of death does not arise. These two statements are complete in themselves; they do not cancel each other. Their dimensions are different, so this always creates difficulties.

The difficulty becomes even more confusing because all my statements are spoken and not written. In statements that are written down there is a sort of indifference. They are not addressed to anyone. The listener or the reader is not sitting opposite while it is written down. The listener or the reader is out of the picture. But when something is spoken, the listener is present and he is also taken into consideration. Thus, whenever I speak about something, I alone am not responsible for the statements. The listener is also responsible.

Responsibility, therefore, is shared. I am definitely responsible for the statements, but the listener is also responsible for creating a situation that called for the statements being made in a particular manner. If another listener had been there, my statements might have been different; in the presence of a third one, they might have again been different; if my statements were unaddressed to anyone, they might have been different again.

All my statements are addressed, and all spoken words are more alive. They receive life from the speaker as well as the listener. When there is no listener, then the speaker is making a sort of bridge toward something that is not there. There is no other bank for the bridge to reach across to. But how can there be a bridge without two banks? There cannot be. A bridge standing on one bank is bound to fall.

Therefore, in this world, all the significant statements about truth are spoken and not written. If I write anything, I write letters, because a letter is as good as something that is spoken. It is addressed. I have not written anything except letters, because to me they are a manner of speaking. The other is always there before me when I write a letter.

Thus, when I speak before thousands of people at a time, then the statements are multiplied in thousands. When these are reproduced by someone, he also includes himself in the statements he reproduces. This creates more and more difficulties, but that is as it is and I am not interested in making any attempt to do something about it. I am interested that you too fully understand the difficulty. If you understand the complexity of a revealed truth, only then will you grow.

I am, therefore, not interested in reducing this complexity, because in attempting to do so the wholeness of the truth is destroyed. It can be simplified, but then a few of its limbs may be severed. Then it will be as good as dead. So I am not in the least interested in reducing its complexity. My only interest is that you should find the simplicity right in the heart of the complexity. Then you will grow.

If I want, I can make the complexity appear simple. There is no difficulty in that. Then my statements will become clear and mathematical and then my difficulties will be over. But I am not worried about my difficulties; they are not difficulties at all. But if you can see simplicity in complexity, if you can see the truth with its contradictions, if you can see the consistency in inconsistencies, then there is growth and your vision will be raised. And only if your vision is raised will you see it. Then only will the complexity become simple for you.

While climbing a mountain, we see several paths on the way up – difficult, steep paths, cutting through each other. But upon reaching the top, the same paths appear easy. When you can see everything in its totality, in one expanse, you see that all the paths are running toward the peak. Neither do they cut each other off, nor do they run against each other. When someone is climbing up, all other paths except his seem to be going the wrong way. But when one who is looking down from the top of the mountain says that all paths are leading to the top, or when he tells one person that this path is right and another person that it is wrong, then it creates confusion.

All my statements are addressed to someone; each of my statements has its proper address. Such statements are for the benefit of a particular person in terms of his particular circumstances. If I see a person with a divided mind on a certain path, and I tell him that this path is right and that other paths are wrong, then that statement is only for his benefit. After reaching the top, he will also know and will laugh upon seeing that other paths are also coming up.

However, if after reaching half way to the top he finds by his side another path ascending and begins to walk upon it, and if a little later he finds a third path ascending and attempts to go on that as well, he may not reach the top at all with such an uncertain, divided mind. To such a person I will have to say, "You are on the right path. Keep on going; other paths are wrong." But if another person on a nearby path is also in a similar situation, is also of a divided mind, I will tell him the same thing: that his path is the right one. If these two persons ever happen to meet and compare these two different statements, it will create difficulties.

Buddha and Mahavira did not have to face a situation like this. Their statements were not recorded in their presence. And after five hundred years their followers were in trouble because of this. The question which you are asking of me could not be asked of Buddha.

After five hundred years, therefore, different sects came into being. Statements had been spoken but were not recorded, so there was no way of comparing them. One thing was told to one person, another thing to another, a third thing to a third, but none of the three recorded anything. Therefore, there was no opportunity to find out by comparing that one person was told this, another was told that and a third was told something altogether different. These statements were made to three different people privately, for their personal benefit. But when they were written down, problems began cropping up.

That is why, for a long time, old religions insisted upon not preparing any scriptures. When things are recorded, the contradictions become clear. As soon as they are written down, questioning will start. At first the statements are personal. Immediately after they are written down, they cease to be personal.

So the difficulty which I am facing was not faced by Buddha and Mahavira. But now there is no way out. Now, whatever is spoken will be recorded, even though it was addressed to a particular person. After it is recorded, it will become the property of the society. Then all those statements made at different times to different people will be gathered together, and it will be difficult to find a single thread of consistency.

Now, this is how it must happen; there is no other way. And

I think it is good. If statements were recorded in Buddha's presence, he could have replied to them. But they were written down only after five hundred years. Then, when questions arose, there was no Buddha to reply. The result was that one person who believed one statement to be true founded his own sect, while another who believed that the contradictory statement was true established another sect. Whoever had a statement established a sect. All sects are born in this manner.

With me there is no possibility of any sect being born. I can be asked directly for clarification. There is no necessity to wait until tomorrow; it can be cleared up today.

You have also asked me to clarify why, though I speak in words, I still maintain that nothing can be conveyed by words. For those who want to speak, there is no other way except by using words. Ordinarily, I can express what I want to say only in words, but it is also true that what has to be said cannot be conveyed by words. Both of these things are true. Our situation is such that we can speak only with words. There is no other way for a dialogue.

We should try to change this situation. For those who can go into deep meditation, dialogue is possible even without words. But to take them into deep meditation, first I will have to use words. A time will come, after a long continued effort, when communication will be possible without words. But until that time comes, I will have to express through words.

To carry you into the wordless world, I will have to use words; this is the situation. But it is full of danger also. I will have to speak in words, knowing full well that if you cling to the words, if you believe in them as they are, then all the trouble we are taking will become useless. We are trying to reach the wordless, but we must speak in words. It is sheer helplessness; there is no other alternative. If you cling to the words, the whole effort becomes useless because the purpose is to take you into wordlessness. While speaking only in words we will have to speak against words, and in that speaking against we will also have to use words. There is no other way.

One can become silent; there is no difficulty. There are those who became silent because of this difficulty. They avoided complications, but they knew that what they had to tell could not be communicated.

I have no difficulty in becoming silent. I can become silent, and it will not be surprising if I become so because what I am trying to do seems to be a nearly impossible effort. I am trying to make the impossible possible. But by my becoming silent nothing can be achieved, nothing can be communicated to you. The danger is the achieved, nothing can be communicated to you. The danger is the same.

If I speak, you will cling to the words. The danger is that if you cling to the words, what I want to communicate and achieve will not happen. But if I become silent, there is no question of communicating anything. In the first instance, if I talk, there is the possibility that what I have said will reach some people. If I talk to a hundred persons, there will be at least one who may perhaps receive what I have said without clinging to the words. For the other ninety-nine, the effort will be useless. Let it be so! This way at least something can be communicated to one, but if I become silent even that one possibility is not there. Therefore, my effort continues.

It is interesting to note that one who believes that things can be communicated by words does not speak much. He speaks a little, and that is the end of it. But one who believes that things cannot be expressed in words will speak much, because howsoever much he may speak, he knows that what he has to say has not yet been communicated. He will speak again and again and again.

This speaking by Buddha over a long period, morning and evening daily for forty years, was not because he thought that by words things can be expressed or communicated. It was because every time, after speaking, he felt that what had to be said had still not been communicated. So Buddha would speak again. He would speak in some different way, in some different manner, in different words. That is why forty years were passed in speaking.

But then the fear remains that if I speak for so long a period as forty years, it may happen that people will hold onto my words only. Because for forty years my method of giving is through words, I have to go on shouting, "Do not cling to my words!" This is a peculiar situation. However, there is no way out of it.

For taking one beyond words, words will have to be used, there is no other way. The situation is something like this: there is a room, and in order to go out of this room, five to ten steps will have to be taken within the room itself. From where we are sitting, five or ten steps have to be taken to go out. Someone may ask, "By walking within the room, how can one go out of it?" Everything depends on how you walk in the room.

If a person walks around and around in the room, he may walk for miles and he will not come out of the room. But a person can walk directly toward the door also – not in a circle, but in a straight line. If while walking he walks in a circle, he will merely walk around the room. If he walks in a straight line toward the door, he can walk out through the door also. But in both of these cases he will be walking only in the room.

If I tell a person who has taken many rounds in the room that he can take just ten steps and he will be out of the room, he will immediately ask me whether I have gone mad. He will say, "You are talking of taking only ten steps, but I have been walking for miles and I have not yet come out of the room." He is not saying anything false, but he has simply been going around and around.

It is interesting to note that in this world everything is going around and around. Our movement is circular. All movement is circular. Unless you make an effort, things will move circularly. To walk straight requires considerable effort.

In this world, all movement is circular. Whether it is an atom or a room or the life of a man or a thought, everything moves around and around in this world. Walking straight requires an effort; walking straight is itself a great achievement.

You do not realize at what moment you begin to walk in a circle. That is why geometry says that a straight line cannot be drawn. All straight lines are only parts of a big circle. We have an illusion of lines being straight, but there is no such thing as a straight line in this world. A straight line cannot be drawn; it is only a definition. Euclid said that the straight line is just a definition. It is imaginary; it cannot be drawn. Howsoever straight a line we may draw, we can only draw it on the earth. As the earth is round, the line will also be round. We can draw a straight line in this room, but it is only a part of a larger circle of the earth.

Is it a curve?

IT is such a small curve that we cannot see it. But if we go on extending it on either end, we will find that it is really a circle that goes around the world. We will find that the straight line has become round; that is why it is impossible to draw a straight line.

When we think about it deeply, the greatest problem in meditation is that all thinking is circular. Even our consciousness moves in a circle. What is most arduous, what is the greatest *tapascharya,* austerity, is to take a jump out of this circular movement. But there seems no way out.

Words also move in a circle. We never have any idea about how words can be circular, but words *are* circular. When you define a word, you make use of other words. If you open a dictionary and see the word 'man', you will find the meaning is 'human being'. If you then look for the word 'human', the meaning is 'having the qualities of man'. What is all this? It is a great madness. We do not know how to define man or human being. What does this mean?

Those who refer to dictionaries do not have any idea that dictionaries are circular. One word is used to define a second word and the second word is used to define the first. A man is a human being and a human being is a man. Where is the definition of man? Thus, all definitions are circular; all principles are circular. To explain one principle you use another, and to explain the other you use the first. Our consciousness is circular. That is why in old age we behave like children. The circle is complete.

No matter how much words may be spoken, they move only

in a circle. Words go around; they cannot walk straight. If you walk straight, you will walk out of them into wordlessness. But because we are living in words, if I have something to say against words I will have to use words to say it. This is a type of madness, but I am not at fault. I speak in the knowledge that without words you cannot understand, and then I speak against words in the hope that you will not cling to them. If this happens, then only will I be able to convey what I want.

If you understand only my words, you will miss what I have said. You will have to understand my words, but along with this, whatever is indicated by them about the wordless world will also have to be understood. Therefore, I will go on speaking against the scriptures even though what I am saying may itself become a scripture. All scriptures are made like that. There is not a single valuable scripture in which you will not find statements against words. That means there is no scripture which doesn't contain statements against scriptures themselves, whether it is the Gita or the Koran or the Bible, or even with Mahavira or Buddha.

There is no reason to believe that something different will happen with me. The same impossible effect will continue. While speaking over and over again against words, I will have spoken many words. Someone or other may catch hold of them and make scriptures out of them. But I cannot stop speaking because there is one chance in a hundred of them becoming a scripture. Only if I stop speaking will there be a safeguard against this one chance. However, there is no basis for this fear, because someone will come along after a while who will speak against my words and the scriptures that will have been made from them. There need be no fear!

But a strange thing happens here and that is this: In the future, my work in this world will be furthered by the very person who speaks against me. Today it is like this: if one wants to work in favor of Buddha, he will have to speak against Buddha. Buddha's words have been picked up by many like old stones, and these stones cannot be removed until Buddha is removed. With the deification of Buddha, these stones have lodged themselves inside the chests of the people who have picked them up. If the stones are to be removed, Buddha will also have to be pulled down; otherwise the stones will remain.

Now you can understand my helplessness. You can understand why I have to speak against Buddha, even though I know full well that I am doing his work. But how else can those who cling to the name of Buddha or the words of Buddha be moved? Until Buddha is moved they cannot be moved. In order to move them we have to take the trouble of disturbing Buddha unnecessarily.

As long as the Vedas are not cast off, there is no way of moving such people. They cling to the Vedas. As long as a man is not convinced that the Vedas are useless, he will not drop them. If for once and for all the mind can be emptied, something further can be done.

But after this emptying process I will say the same things that the Vedas have said. Then the difficulties increase further. False friends and false enemies unnecessarily come into being. As things are, ninety-nine times out of a hundred one meets false friends and false enemies. A false friend is one who will take what I speak to be scriptures, and the false enemy is one who believes that what I speak is against the scriptures and that I am an enemy of the scriptures. But things are like this, it will inevitably happen like this, and there is no need to worry about it. Such is the situation.

So You do not want to write?

NO, I do not want to write. There are many reasons why I do not want to write. For one thing, it is absurd and useless to write. It is useless because for whom shall I write? To me, writing appears to be like writing a letter without knowing the address. How can I enclose it in an envelope and dispatch it when I do not know the address?

A statement is always addressed. Those who want to address the masses write. This is the way they address the unknown crowd.

But the more unknown the crowd, the fewer are the things that can be said. And the nearer or more known the individual addressed is, the deeper can be the dialogue.

Deeper truths can only be told to a particular person. To a crowd, only temporary, simple things can be told. The bigger the crowd, the lesser the understanding, and the more unknown the crowd, the more one has to proceed with a presumption that there will be no understanding. Thus, the more literature is meant for the masses, the more down to earth and simple it will be. Flying in the skies is not possible with this kind of literature.

If you find delicate nuances of meaning in the poetry of Kalidas and you do not find them in the poetry of modern poets, it is not due to any difference between Kalidas and the modern poet. It is because Kalidas' poetry is addressed and recited in the presence of an emperor or a few selected persons, while the modern poem is printed in a newspaper. The newspaper may be read while taking tea in a tea shop, while eating peanuts, while smoking. The poem may just be glanced at. Who then is it being written for? The modern poet does not care to know. He must write for everyman, for the lowest common denominator. He must keep everyman in view while writing.

My difficulty is that even to those who are the best amongst us, it is difficult to relate truth. To those who are less than the best, to the common man, the question of relating truth does not arise. Only those of us who are among the chosen few can understand the deepest matters. But even among this chosen few, ninety-nine out of a hundred will miss what I have said. So there is no meaning in telling such things to a crowd, and writing is done only for a crowd.

There are also other reasons for not writing. I believe that as the medium one uses changes, the content also changes. With the change of medium, the subject matter does not remain the same. The medium poses its own conditions and changes on what is said.

This is not easily understandable. When I am speaking, this is one type of medium. The whole line of communication is alive. The listener is living and I am also living. When I am speaking the listener not only listens: he also sees. The changing expressions of my face, the minute changes reflected in my eyes, the raising and falling of my finger, are all seen by him. Not only does he listen to my words: he also sees the movement of my lips. It is not only my words that speak, it is also my lips that speak. My eyes also say something. All of this is taken in by the listener. The content of what I have said will be different in a listener's mind than in a reader's mind because all of this will have become a part of it.

When someone reads a book, then in place of me there are only black letters and black ink, nothing else. I and the black ink are not equivalents. There is no give and take. In the type, no gestures or changes of expression ever appear, no scenes or pictures are ever created. There is no life; it is a dead message. When one is reading a book, a very significant part of the message which remains alive while I am speaking is lost. In the reader's hands there are only dead statements.

It is interesting to note that a reader can be less attentive than a listener has to be. When a person listens, the degree of attention he is paying is far greater than when he reads. While listening one must give full attention and concentration, because what has been already spoken will not be repeated. You cannot revive parts not understood or partly understood; they are lost. Every moment that I am speaking, that which is spoken becomes lost in a bottomless abyss. If you have caught it, you have caught it. Otherwise it flows away and it will not return.

While reading a book there is no such fear, because you can re-read the same pages over and over again. There is no necessity, therefore, to be very attentive while reading a book. That is why the day words began to be written down was the day attention became lessened. It was bound to be so.

With a book, if you have not understood something you can turn back the page and read it again. But with my speaking it is not possible to go back. What is missed is lost. The knowledge of what is spoken is lost forever if missed and cannot be repeated. This keeps your attention at a full peak. It helps to keep your consciousness at its maximum alertness. When you read at leisure, if something is missed there is no harm; you can read it again. With a book, understanding is less and the need for repetition increases. As attention decreases, understanding also decreases.

Therefore, it is not without reason that Buddha, Mahavira and Jesus all selected speech as the medium for the transmission of their message. They could have written, but they selected this medium. They did it for two reasons: One, because the spoken word is a more all-encompassing medium; more can be said. There are many things attached to words which are lost in writing.

That is why, if you think about it, you will notice that the day films began, novels lost their importance. This is because films made things alive again. Who will read a novel? It is a dead thing. The novel cannot live much longer. It may become lost as an art form because we now have mediums that are more living, what McLuhan calls "hot" mediums. Television and films are live mediums, hot mediums. There is heat in their blood.

But the written word is a cold medium, dead cold. There is no life in it; no blood flows in it. Even your telephone may become outdated as soon as phonovision comes, just as radio began to become outdated with the coming of television. Radio has become a comparatively colder medium while television is a hot medium. And to me speaking is a hot medium; there is blood and heat in it.

So far we have not been able to find enough ways to add emphasis to words that are written. If I want to emphasize something when I am speaking, I can speak a little louder. I can change the nuances in my voice, my voice rhythm; then emphasis is conveyed. But in the words of a book there is no such way. The words are just dead. In a book, the word love *is* love whether it was written by a person making love or by one not making love, or by one living in love or by one who does not know what love is. There are no nuances, no rhythm, no waves, no vibrations. It is dead.

When Jesus says the word prayer, its meaning is not the same as when someone writes the same word in a book. The whole life of Jesus is a prayer, from beginning to end. Every particle of him is prayer; every inch of his body is filled with it. Thus, what Jesus conveys when he says the word prayer is very different from what is conveyed by the word in a dictionary.

Whenever one speaks, it immediately creates a sort of tuning in, a getting in touch with the listener. The soul of the speaker soon approaches that of the listener. Doors open up; the listener's defenses begin to give way.

When you are listening, if you are fully attentive your thinking has to stop. The more attentive you are as you listen, the less you will think. Your doors open; you become more receptive to the other. Now something can enter in directly without being hindered; you and the speaker become known to each other. In a very deep sense, a harmonious relationship is established. The speaking comes from without, yet it echoes deep within the listener.

Such a relationship cannot be established when one is reading, because the writer is absent. When you are reading, if you do not automatically understand something you have to make an attempt to understand it. But when listening you will understand without effort.

If you are reading a book based on my speaking that has been reported verbatim, then you will forget that you are reading because you know me. After a few moments, you feel that you are not reading – that you are listening. But if the wording is changed or the style is changed slightly in the reporting, the rhythm and the attunement will break. When those who have listened to me read my spoken words, reading becomes as good as listening to me. But there are differences because, still, a change in medium changes the intent of what is said.

The difficulty is that what I am trying to tell will change in accordance with the form of expression. If I use poetry, it will impose its own conditions: a particular arrangement of words, the rejection or selection of particular subject matter, the breaking off or cutting out of particular things. If it is necessary to express the same thing in prose, the content will be entirely different.

That is why, for the most part, all of the great books in the world have been written in the form of poetry. What was being told was so beyond logic that it was difficult to express it in prose form. Prose is very logical; poetry is very illogical. Lack of logic is permitted and forgiven in poetry, but not in prose. In poetry, if you go a little beyond the logical understanding in places, you have license to do so. Not so in prose.

Because depth poetry is illogical, depth prose has to be logical. If you try to write the Upanishads or the Gita in prose, you will find that that which makes them alive is lost. The medium has changed, and what was beautiful as poetry will be awkward and bothersome as prose. They are not logical, but prose will try to make them so because prose is an arrangement of logic.

The Upanishads were recited in the form of poetry; so was the Gita. But Buddha and Mahavira did not speak in the form of poetry. There was a reason for this change. Since the time the Upanishads and the Gita were written, the world had changed. The period when they were written was, in one sense, poetical. People were simple and straightforward; there was no demand for logic. If they were told, "God is," they simply said yes; they did not turn around and ask, "What is God? How does he look?"

If you look at the way children are, you will have an idea of what type of people there must have been in those days. A child may ask a very difficult question, yet he will be pleased by a simple answer. The child may ask from where his small sister or brother came. You answer that he or she was brought by a stork and he is satisfied. Then he runs away to play. He had asked a very difficult question to which even the highly intelligent are not able to give a correct answer. The child asked a most basic, ultimate question: "From where do children come?" You answered that the stork brings them, and by the time you have said it the child is already gone. He is pleased with a very simple answer. And the more poetical the answer, the more pleased he will be. That is why in books for small children we have to use poetry. Poetry reaches the child's heart very quickly. There is a rhythm and a melody in it that reaches his mind quickly. A child lives in the world of rhythm and melody.

Buddha and Mahavira used prose because in the time period that they were living people were accustomed to doing a lot of logical thinking. Minute questions were asked, but even with long intricate answers people were not satisfied. Then they would ask twenty-five more questions. That is why Buddha and Mahavira had to speak in prose.

Now it is not possible to speak in poetry any more. Now poetry is written for entertainment. Once all fundamental, serious matters were told only in the form of poetry. But now serious matters cannot be told in poetic form. Those few people who have some leisure and the desire to entertain you still write poetry, but all matters of value will be told in prose only. Man is no longer like a child; he has become an adult. He thinks logically on all matters. Only prose can be used logically.

Each medium changes the content. To my mind, as methods of communication develop, the conveying of thought through speech will return again. For a while the printed word was the most important, but now technological advances are leading us back to the possibility of direct communication through a living medium, through television.

After a while, nobody will be willing to read a book anymore. I can speak to the whole world on a television network. All can listen directly. Therefore, the future of the book is not very good. Now, in a way, a book will not be read; it will be seen. This will have to be made popular; the book will have to be transformed. Now microfilms have developed, so it is possible to see the book on a screen. Words will very soon be changed to pictures.

In my view writing developed out of helplessness. There was no other way. Even now, those who want to convey something that is very important use the medium of speech. I do not know for whom I would write. As long as there is no one in front of me, no desire arises within me to speak. The pleasure of speaking for the sake of speaking is not there in me.

This is the difference between a writer and one who is enlightened. The litterateur has a sort of interest in just expressing something. He is pleased if he can do so. A big burden seems to drop from his shoulders when he does so.

In me there is no such burden. When I am speaking to you I am not receiving pleasure just because I am telling you something. In telling something, there is no feeling of being relieved of a burden. My telling, in a sense, is less an expression and more a response.

There is no feeling in me that I have to tell you something. If you want to know something, only then will it occur to me to say something. The condition of my mind is such that if you throw a bucket in my well something will emerge from it. It is gradually becoming difficult for me to speak unless a question has been asked. In the future, it is going to be more and more difficult for me just to speak. Therefore, I have to find excuses.

I need an excuse if I am to speak on the Gita. If you create such an excuse, then I will speak. But it is becoming difficult for me to speak if you do not provide the excuse. If there is no nail or peg on which to hang something, on what to hang it and why I should hang it is a problem. I remain silent – empty. You go out of this room and I become empty.

If someone has the desire to speak, the need to speak, then he will make himself ready to speak even when you are not in the room. His mind will prepare what to say even though there is no one present. When enough material accumulates in him, he will be impelled to speak.

For me this is not true. I am completely empty. If you raise a question and make me speak, only then will I speak. That is why writing is difficult. Writing is easier for those who are full.

Why do You not write Your autobiography?

THIS can also be asked – why I do not write my autobiography. It may seem very interesting, but truly speaking after self-knowledge there is no autobiography. All autobiographies are ego-biographies. What we call an autobiography is not the story of the soul. As long as you do not know what soul is, whatever you write is ego-biography.

It is interesting to note that neither Jesus, nor Krishna, nor Buddha have written their autobiographies. They neither told them nor wrote them. Writing or speaking about oneself has not been possible for those who have known themselves, because after knowing the person changes into something so formless that what we call the facts of his life – facts like the date he was born, the date a particular event happened – dissolve. What happens is that all these facts cease to have any meaning. The awakening of a soul is so cataclysmic that after it occurs, when one opens his eyes he finds that everything is lost. Nothing is left; no one remains to talk about what has happened.

After one has known one's soul, an autobiography seems to be a dreamlike version of oneself. It is as if one were writing an account of his dreams: One day he saw this dream, the next day that dream, and the day after that a third dream. Such an autobiography has no more value than a fantasy, a fairy tale.

That is why it is difficult for an awakened person to write. On becoming awakened and aware, he finds that there is nothing worth writing. It was all a dream. The matter of the experience of becoming aware remains, but what is known through the experience cannot be written down. This is so because reducing such an experience to words makes it seem insipid and absurd. Even so, there is always the attempt to tell about the experience in different ways through different methods.

My whole life I shall go on telling what has happened. There is nothing else to tell except this. But this also cannot be written down. As soon as it is written, it is felt that it was not worth talking about. What is there to write? One may write, "I have had an experience of the soul. I am full of joy and peace." But it looks absurd – mere words.

Buddha, Mahavira and Christ went on telling their whole lives in many different ways what they had known. They never became tired. They always felt that there was still something left out, so they would speak again in a different way. It is never finished. Buddha and Mahavira may finish, but what they have to tell remains incomplete.

The problem is twofold: what can be told seems like a dream and only what cannot be told seems worth saying. There always remains lurking in the mind the feeling that if I tell you what has happened to me it is of no use. My purpose is to take you on that path that may lead you to the experience itself. Only then can you someday understand what has happened to me. Before that you cannot understand it, and my telling you what has happened to me directly serves no purpose. I don't think you will believe what I say. And what is the use of my making you suspicious? It will be harmful. The best way is to take you on that path, to that bank from which you can be pushed to where someday you yourself may have the experience. On that day you will be able to trust. You will know the way it happens. Otherwise there is no way to trust.

At the time of the death of Buddha people asked, "Where will you go after death?" What does Buddha reply? He says, "I have been nowhere, so where can I go after death? I have never gone anywhere and have never been anywhere." Even after this people still asked him where he would go, but he had told the truth because the meaning of buddhahood is nowhereness. In that state one is nowhere, so the question of being somewhere does not arise.

If you can be quiet and silent, what remains except breathing? Only breathing remains; nothing else. Like the air inside a bubble, breathing remains. If you can be silent at least once for a few moments, then you will realize that when there are no thoughts there is nothing but breathing. The inhaling and exhaling of air is nothing more than the going out and coming in of air in a bubble or a balloon. So Buddha says, "I was only a bubble. Where was I? A bubble has burst and you are asking where it has gone." If someone like Buddha knows that he is like a bubble, how can he write his autobiography or tell about his experience? Whatever he might say will be misunderstood.

In Japan there was one saint called Lin Chi. One day Lin Chi ordered the removal of all the idols of Buddha. There had never been a man like him. Only just before he had been worshipping those very idols of Buddha, and now he was ordering them to be removed. Someone stood up and asked, "Are you in your right mind? Do you know what you are saying?"

Lin Chi answered, "As long as I was thinking that I am, I believed that Buddha was. But when I myself am not there, when I am only an air bubble, then I know that someone like Buddha also could not have been there."

In the evening Lin Chi was again worshipping Buddha. People again asked him what he was doing. He said, "I was helped in my own non-being by Buddha's non-being. That is why I have been giving thanks. It was a thanksgiving from one bubble to another, nothing more." But these statements could not be properly understood. People thought that there was something wrong with this man and that he had gone against Buddha.

Autobiography does not survive. Deeply speaking, the soul itself does not survive. So far, we understand only that the ego does not survive. For thousands of years, we have been told that the ego does not survive. For thousands of years, we have been told that the ego does not survive when one attains self-knowledge. But to put it correctly, the soul itself does not survive.

In understanding this one is filled with fear. That is why we could not understand Buddha. He said, "The soul also does not survive; we become non-soul." It becomes very difficult to understand Buddha in this world.

Mahavira talked only of the death of the ego; that much could be understood. It is not that Mahavira did not know that even the soul does not survive, but he had in mind our limited understanding. Therefore, he spoke only of giving up the ego, knowing that the soul would automatically dissolve.

Buddha, for the first time, made a statement which had been a secret. The Upanishads also knew, Mahavira also knew, that the soul does not survive in the end, because the idea of the soul is a projection of the ego. But Buddha revealed the secret which had been closely guarded for so long. That created difficulties. Those who themselves believed that the ego does not survive started the quarrel. If the soul does not survive either, they said, then everything is useless. Where are we?

Buddha was right. How could there be an autobiography then? Everything is like a dream sequence, like the rainbow colors formed on a bubble. The colors die when the bubble bursts. That is a very obvious result.

Will the processes and experiences through which a person has passed be of any use to others if they are written down?

IT may be useful for the seeker, but it is very difficult for the enlightened one to write it. The difficulties of the *siddha,* the enlightened one, are different from those of the *sadhak,* the seeker. The difficulty is that for the enlightened one there are no spirits in this room, but for you there are. The siddha knows that the spirits do not exist, but at one time he too had a spirit which he exorcised with the help of a technique. Now he knows that both the spirit and the technique were false.

Knowing this, how can he say that he had driven away the spirit with the help of the technique? Do you follow me? This is a problem for the master. He knows that the spirit was false and that the technique was just a help in the darkness. The spirit was false and so also was the technique that drove it away. So how can he say that he drove away the spirit with the technique? To say so now is meaningless. But if he could say that he drove away the spirit with the technique, it would be a help to you.

The master will not say that he drove away the spirit by the power of the technique. Rather, he will say that "spirits can be made to disappear by the use of certain techniques. If the seeker uses such and such a technique the spirit will go." The master will not say that he drove away the spirit with a technique because it would be a false statement. Now he knows that the technique was as false as the spirit.

Therefore, the statements of such a person will be least self-centered. He will hardly ever speak about himself. He talks about you and what is relevant to your situation, so it is his problem that in order to help you he will have to make a false statement.

Do You mean that the whole 'sadhana' process, the process of spiritual practice, is as unreal as a ghost?

YES, it is, because what you ultimately achieve has always been with you and that from which you are freed has never bound you. But this presents a difficulty for the master; that is why I say that the master has his own difficulties. If he says that the whole *sadhana* process is false, then he will put you in difficulty, because for you the process becomes false while the spirit remains real. Even a false process is meaningful if it serves the purpose of making the spirit false. Do you follow me?

A spirit does not become false just by calling it false. It is interesting to note that a wrong thing does not cease to be wrong just by calling it right, but when something that is right is called wrong we immediately accept it. No matter how much one says that anger is wrong, that does not make it wrong.

On the other hand, if someone says meditation is wrong, you immediately feel that it may be so; it does not even take a second to become wrong. You do not immediately agree when it is claimed that a particular person is a saint, but if you are told that someone is a thief you immediately accept it as the truth.

Before you are willing to believe that a person is a saint, you will try to test him, you will try to prove in various ways whether this is so. The reason you are so cautious is that it makes you uneasy if someone else is said to be a saint. Your ego is hurt. You will try to prove that he is no more a saint than you are. When you are told that someone else is a thief, you do not bother to test it; you believe it immediately because believing it makes you happy. It assures you that you are not the only thief, that someone else is at least as bad as you are.

Slander and condemnation of another are easily accepted, but it is not so with praise. Even when you accept someone as being praiseworthy, even if you yourself really know that he is so, the acceptance is still conditional. You accept it for the time being because you have no other choice, but you continue to look for an opportunity to change your opinion. Only condemnation is absolute. Even if something happens to make you change a negative opinion, you will not bother to do so.

This happens all the time in life. When something is claimed to be wrong, we immediately believe it because this saves us from doing what is right. One must be very determined if he is going to continue to do what is right. Anger is spontaneous; we continue to express it even if we have been told it is wrong. But meditation must be practiced, and this is much more difficult. So if someone says that meditation is something bogus, we feel relieved at being saved from doing something arduous.

You have described meditation not as an action, but as a state of being. Will You explain this?

THE difficulty for the enlightened person is that if he tells you everything he has experienced, you will lose the path forever because what he says will be so far removed from your experience. For example, I have described meditation as a state of being. What I say is true, and yet for you meditation can only be an activity, not a state. If you believe it is a state of being, you will feel that there is nothing you can do to achieve it. If it is an activity, then you are required to do something; if it is merely a state of consciousness, then you are relieved of the need to act.

You will think, "Perhaps it is a state of being. Then there is nothing that I can do about it." Then your anger will continue and you will not do any meditation. Your sex, your greed will continue.

If I tell the truth, you are not helped by me. The difficulty is that if I say something keeping you in mind, I have to take recourse to telling what is not entirely true. But if I say something keeping myself in mind, it is useless for you. It is not only useless; it is also dangerous because you happen to be the listener. Deep down it will be a hindrance to you if I tell you the complete truth exactly as I see it.

That is why, if I say exactly what I feel, I cannot be of any help to you. On the contrary, what I would say would be a hindrance to you, like Krishnamurti's talks which hinder people's progress more than they help it. The deeper I look, the more I feel that such talks are harmful. What he is saying is the inner truth, but for you it is not helpful. For you it is only an excuse to stop doing anything.

Is silence very powerful, and if so, then why should anybody speak in words?

YES, silence is very powerful, but first there must be people who can hear what is conveyed in silence.

Why is it necessary to make people listen?

IT is necessary to me because I see that you are moving unknowingly toward a deep pit, and it is clear to me that you will fall into the pit and break your hands or feet. I can convey this fact to you in silence. But your ears cannot hear my silent message, so I have to shout at you to warn you, "Be careful! You will fall into the pit."

Do You lose any energy by doing so?

NO, no! No energy is lost. One who has known the source of energy does not lose energy. Only one who does not know the source can lose.

If I write anything like an autobiography, it may be either truth or untruth. If it is truth, it may harm you. If it is untruth, I would not want to write it. If it is completely truthful, it will cause you harm because I will have to say that whatever you are doing now is useless. You will readily agree with me that it is so.

One day an individual came to me. He said, "Because Krishnamurti said that meditation is useless, I have stopped doing meditation."

I said, "You have done a good thing. But what did you gain from it? You did not gain anything. Why did you start doing meditation in the first place? You wanted to conquer your anger and ignorance. Did you accomplish that by giving up meditation? No! Then why did you stop? Because Krishnamurti said that it is useless!"

You feel, "When a realized person says it is useless, why should I continue to do it?" This is the difficulty: I also know that it is useless; I also tell this to some, that it is useless. But I will only say this to a person who has done meditation for a long time and who can now understand its uselessness. Such a person has reached a stage where meditation must also be given up.

But to say in the marketplace that meditation is useless is dangerous. The listeners may have never done any meditation. Those ignorant people have never done it. If you tell them that meditation is useless, they will never do it. They will feel very much relieved. For forty years people are listening to Krishnamurti, and they are sitting around foolishly doing nothing just because Krishnamurti said that meditation is useless. Krishnamurti is not wrong when he says so. He has been saying it for his whole life. But I would say he is wrong because he is not keeping you and your capacity in mind. He is only talking about his own experiences.

It is because of this that I am always very careful, that I do not project myself and do not say anything about myself. If I talk about myself and only say the truth, it will be of no use to you. It is strange that if I talk about you, keeping you in mind, then you will come back to me and ask, "Why did you tell such things?" Then there comes opposition. I can say things which can never be opposed, but these things will be of no use to you. They may give you an excuse to stop where you are.

The difficulty of the enlightened one is that he is not able to tell what he knows. Therefore, in one way, old tradition was much more correct and went much deeper. You were told something according to where you were at the time. All information was tentative; nothing was ultimate. As you made progress the master would give you new things; as you progressed further, it would be said, "Now give up this, give up that. It has become useless."

When you reached the appropriate state, you were told that God is useless, the soul is useless, meditation is useless – but just on that day, not before. But this can be told only at that moment when these things become useless; then nothing is *really* useless. Then you just laugh and you know.

If I say meditation is useless and you still continue to do meditation, then I will feel that you were the right person to be told – that it was good that I told you. If I say sannyas is useless – that taking sannyas is useless – and still you become initiated into it, I will understand that you were the right sort of person to be told. It was good.

So these things which I have spoken about are the sort of difficulties I face. All this will be understood slowly and gradually.

2

WHY I HAVE COME

March 7, 1971

You said that if one were talking about the body You would say that the body was death-oriented and if one were talking about the soul You would say, "You were never born at all." Buddha has said of the soul, "It was just a bubble which is now no more. I myself am not there, so where will I go?" Then what is it that is immortal and who is unborn?

THERE is a sea over which waves come and go, but the sea remains the same. The waves are not separate from the sea, but the waves are not the sea. Waves are only forms born on the sea, just appearances which take form and die. A wave that remains a wave forever cannot be called a wave. The word 'wave' means it dies as soon as it is born. That from which the wave arises is always there, but that which arises is not. This is a dance of the transitory on the breast of the eternal. The sea is unborn; the wave is taking birth. The sea never dies; the wave always dies. The moment the wave knows that it is the sea, it goes beyond the chain of life and death. But as long as the wave believes that it is a wave it is within the possibility of birth and death.

That which is, is unborn and deathless. From where will birth come? Nothing is born out of the void. Where will death happen?

Nothing is lost in the void. That which is, is eternal. Time makes no difference to it; time does not affect it. This existence is not within our grasp because our senses can only comprehend form and shape. Our senses cannot comprehend that which is beyond name and form.

It is interesting to note that you must have stood on the shore of the sea very often and upon returning would have said that you have seen the sea. But you have only seen the waves, not the sea. The sea cannot be seen. What you can see are the waves. Senses can see only what appears on the surface. That which is within remains beyond their comprehension. The senses see the superficial form; the formless within eludes their grasp.

The world of name and form is born only because of the senses. It is not existence. Whatsoever has a name and form is born and will die and that which is beyond name and form is eternal. Neither is it born, nor will it die. So when Buddha says that he was born as a bubble, he is referring to two aspects of a bubble. What does the bubble contain? If we enter into a bubble, we will find that a very small amount of the same infinite all-pervasive air that is outside is enclosed within a thin film of water. This thin film has imprisoned a small portion of air, and that small part of air has become the bubble.

Naturally, like everything, the bubble also expands. Upon expanding, it breaks and bursts. Then the air that was within the bubble unites with the outer air and the water with water. But that which came into existence meanwhile was a rainbow existence. Nothing ever changed in the air or the water; they remain as they are. But meanwhile, a form was born which died.

If we look upon ourselves as bubbles, then we also are forms that take birth and die. What is within us was always, but we identify ourselves with the bubble. So if I am looking at you from the point of view of the body, I will say that you are death-oriented and slowly dying. From the moment you were born you began dying, and you have not been doing anything else except dying. The bubble may take seven moments to burst, but you take about seventy years to burst.

In the endless flow of time, there is no difference between seven moments and seventy years. All difference is due to our narrow vision. If time is endless with no beginning and no end, then what is the difference between seven moments and seventy years? If time is a determined quantity, say a hundred years, then seven moments will be very small and seventy years will be quite a long span. But if there is no limit on either end, if there is neither a beginning nor an end, then there is no difference between seven moments and seventy years. In how many moments the bubble bursts is of no consequence.

No sooner is it born when it starts bursting. That is why I described the body as death-oriented. By body I mean that which manifests through birth with a name and form. By soul I mean that which remains even after that name and form are lost. When there was no such name and form, then also it was. By the soul I mean the sea and by the body I mean the wave. It is necessary to understand these things clearly.

That which is within us never dies, so inwardly we feel that "I will never die." We see that hundreds of thousands of people are dying but still we are not convinced that we will also die. In our deepest depths there is no echo that "I too will die." People die before our very eyes and still that inner feeling of immortality remains. In deeper moments we are always aware that "I will die." We know that the facts show the fallaciousness of this belief and that outer events indicate that it is not possible that "I will not die." Reason says that if everything else has to die, then you will also die. But some voice within severs all links with reason and goes on saying, "I will not die."

That is why we do not believe that we will ever die. That is why we are able to live in the midst of death; otherwise, as we are surrounded by death constantly, we would die instantly. Why are we so confident and certain of living? That confidence is due to that something within that goes on telling us that we will not die, regardless of how much we may say, or the occurrence of an actual death may say, that we will die.

No person can ever conceive of his own death. He cannot imagine that he will die. However much he may try to imagine that he is dying, he will find himself still there. Even if he imagines himself dead, he will find that *he* is there seeing, that *he* is there standing outside of death. We are not able to place ourselves within the jaws of death even in imagination, because while imagining we go on watching from the outside. The one who imagines stands outside, so he will not be able to die.

This voice from within is the voice of the sea. It asks us, "Where is death?" Death is unknown; still we are afraid of death. This fear comes from the voice of the body, and there is a confusion between the two. The moment we identify ourselves with the voice of the body, our spirits begin to tremble over the fact that the body is bound to die. No matter how much we may try to disprove this or seek the help of science or devise a system of medicine or surround ourselves with eminent physicians and medicines, the body does not for a single moment confirm that "I will live." The body does not have that feeling of deathlessness; it knows that daily it is dying.

The body knows that it is a bubble, but we know that *we* are not bubbles. The moment one identifies oneself with the bubble, all the tensions of one's life begin. No sooner does that within us which is immortal identify itself with the wave when it comes into difficulties. This identification is ignorance; breaking away from this identification is knowledge. Nothing changes; everything remains the same as before. The body remains where it was; the soul also remains where it was. Only the illusion disappears. Then we know that when the body will die we have not to be afraid, because there is no need to be afraid. The body is bound to die. It is useful to be afraid when there is a possibility of being saved. But in a situation from which there is no possibility of being saved, it is useless to become afraid.

When a soldier marches forward to the battlefield, when he first leaves his house, he is filled with fear. On the battlefield too he is fearful. But when the bombs begin showering upon him he becomes fearless, because then all possibilities of being saved are destroyed. Such a person can even play cards amidst continuous shellfire. And he is an ordinary man; there is nothing special about him. But this is a unique situation. In this situation, fear of death is meaningless. Death is so imminent that there is no question of survival.

On the battlefield, there is some possibility of survival because some die while others survive, and so some fear remains. But on the field of death even that remote possibility is not there. At the moment of death the illusion that "I am the body" suddenly disappears. The fear of death disappears because there is no escape. Then the fact of the body dying becomes a certainty, a destiny. That is the fate of the body; there is no way of saving it.

The moment one realizes that death is the nature of the body, it suddenly becomes apparent that what is beyond the body was never born and so there is no question of its death. Thus, for the soul also, fear vanishes, because there is no reason to be afraid for that which cannot die. The fear arises due to the body and soul becoming identified with each other. It arises because the inner voice says, "I will not die," and the outer voice says, "You will certainly die!" These voices become confused. We are not aware that these two different melodies intermingle, and we listen to them as if they were the melodies of the same instrument. That is the mistake.

In our ignorance there is always a fear of death, but we go on living as if there were no death. Every moment the ignorant person lives as if there were no death though he is frightened of it. The one who knows also lives as if there were no death, but he is aware that death can happen at any moment. He lives at two different levels. Life for him has split into two parts: the circumference has become separate from the center; the wave has become separate from the sea; the form has become separate from the formless. However, one cannot run away from death. It is a matter of wonder that a thing does not by itself cease to appear by our knowing that it is an illusion. By our knowing, only the consequent pain ceases.

Shankaracharya was always giving the example of a rope that appears like a snake in darkness. But this example is inaccurate because by coming near you can know that it is a rope. And once you know that it is a rope, however far from it you may go, it will not look like a snake.

But the illusion of life is not like that. The illusion of life is like a stick that is dipped in water. In the water it will appear bent, but when you remove it from the water, it is straight. If you put it back in the water, it will again look bent. Then if you put your hands in the water you find that the stick is straight, but still it appears bent. Just by your knowing that it is straight, the slanted appearance of the stick does not disappear. But by your knowing, you no longer behave as if in the illusion that it is bent.

Our illusion of life is not like that of a rope looking like a snake, but like that of a straight stick appearing bent in the water. We know full well that the stick is not bent, but only appears so. The stick even appears bent to the greatest of scientists who have experimented and who know that by dipping the stick in water it does not become bent. Thus, this appearance of crookedness is due to our senses. Our knowledge has nothing to do with it.

The difference, therefore, is this: that you will not believe that the stick is bent, but it only appears to be bent. The matter is divided into two different levels. On the level of knowing, the stick is straight. On the level of seeing, it is bent. There is no illusion on either of these levels.

On the level of living there is the body which is the outer and on the level of existence there is the *atma* – the soul. For the knower, the world is not lost. For him the world is just the same as it is for you. Probably, to him the world is clearer in its perspective and appearance. Every tiny cell of the existence is clearer to him. Nothing is lost for him, and he is not in any illusion. He knows that form is born out of the senses and is like the stick which appears bent in water. Because the rays of light bend and change while entering the water, the stick also appears bent. In air, rays of light do not bend, so the stick appears straight. The stick does not bend, but the rays of light bend while passing through water. Therefore, we see the stick as crooked.

The existence is as it is, but while passing through our senses the ray of knowledge becomes bent. The ray of knowledge changes due to the medium through which things are known. If I wear blue spectacles, everything will look blue. When I remove them, I see that everything is white. If I put the spectacles on again, I again see everything as blue. I know that things appear blue due to the spectacles, so I will not be in illusion anymore. But I may continue putting on the specs and things will continue to appear blue. However, though I will know full well that the soul – the being – is immortal, the knowledge that the body is death-oriented also continues.

In spite of my knowing that the existence of the sea is eternal, the play of the waves continues. But now I know that it has appeared so due to the spectacles. The spectacles are the eyes of the senses, and what you see through them is not necessarily real.

That is why the statements of people like Buddha, Mahavira or Jesus are made from two different planes – one of the soul and the other of the body. Our difficulty is that as we are confusing both the planes within ourselves, then naturally we also confuse their statements. Sometimes Buddha speaks as if he were the body. He says, "Ananda, I am thirsty. Please bring me water." The soul is never thirsty. It is the body that feels thirsty. Now Ananda may think that the body is not there at all, that it is only a name and form, just a bubble, "so how can it become thirsty?" Once you have known that there is no body, then from where does thirst come?

Then the next day, when Buddha says, "I am not born at all so I will never die," it creates difficulties for the listener. The listener's difficulty is that he thinks that with knowledge the existence will change. Actually, by knowing the existence does not change; only one's gestalt changes.

When Buddha says that he is thirsty, he only says that his body is thirsty – that this body, which is a bubble of name and form, is thirsty, and if it is not given water it will soon burst. But the listener's difficulty is that because he is living in a confused state, he is not able to distinguish which statement is coming from which plane, so he confuses their meanings also.

Simone Weil has written a book called *Grades of Significance*. The greater the man, the more he lives on different levels of greatness at one time. He has to live like that because he has to talk from the levels of the people he meets. Otherwise, all talk becomes meaningless. If Buddha talks with you from his highest level, it will be useless. You will take him to be mad. It has generally happened that these types of people have been taken as mad. The reason for that is that whatever they said looked as if it were told by a mad person. Thus, if they speak from their level, they will be branded as mad.

If they have to speak from your level, they will have to come down. They will have to come down to a level where you can understand them. Then they will not appear mad. Thus, they will have to talk from as many levels as exist among the people that come to them.

One can say that the many people to whom Buddha spoke would come to him in the form of mirrors. All these mirrors created their own separate images of Buddha, and the images were as faithful as the surfaces of the mirrors themselves. An image must match with the mirror. Thus, a convex mirror will broaden the image while a concave mirror will shorten it. If this were not so, the mirrors would be displeased, and then the mirrors would have to be broken or changed.

That is why the statements of people like Buddha come across on many different levels. Sometimes in only one statement there will be several levels. This is because when a person like Buddha begins to speak he does so from his own level and when he stops speaking he has come down to the level where you are. Many times in only one sentence there is a long journey – because when he begins to speak it is from the level where he is at. He begins with great expectations about you; then slowly he has to bring down his expectations, and in his last statements he reaches where you are.

His level and your level represent two deep divisions, but this does not mean that these two are very distant or separate or different. They are like that of the sea and the wave. The sea can sometimes be without a wave, but the wave can never be without the sea. The formless can be without a form, but a form can never be without the formless.

But if we look at our language, it is interesting to see that it is the reverse. In our language, in the word *nirakar,* formless, there is the word *sakar,* form. But formless is not in the word form. In language, in the word formless, the word form will have to be there; but it will do if the word form does not include the formless. Language is created by us, but in existence the situation is the reverse. In existence there can be the formless without the form, but there can be no form without the formless.

All our words are like that. In the word *ahimsa,* non-violence, the word *himsa,* violence, is necessary. But in the word violence, non-violence is not needed. In life, however, it is interesting to note that in order for violence to exist, non-violence is necessary; it is unavoidable. But non-violence can be there without violence. We create language and we create it according to our needs. For us the world can be without God, but how can God be without a world?

These are not two different things. Therefore, the macrocosmic can exist without the microcosmic; there is no difficulty for the sea to exist without the wave. But how can the wave be without the sea? The wave is very small, and it is dependent for its very being upon the sea. If the surrounding sea raises it, it is there. The sea takes care of it from all the sides. If the sea releases it, it is gone.

These two are not separate, but I have to say that they are separate so that the wave will not be under the illusion that it is immortal, formless and eternal. If the wave thinks itself separate, then there is the possibility for this illusion and its consequences. But if the wave is one with the sea, there is no illusion. If the experience is that of oneness, then it will say, "I am not there at all; there is only the sea." In this way, Jesus was repeatedly saying, "I am not there; only my father in heaven is."

So we are in a difficulty. Either we want to be shown God in heaven so we can find out who he is and where he is, or we will call Jesus mad because we do not understand what he was saying. Jesus was saying, "I am the sea, not the wave," but we have not seen anything else but the wave. Sea is only a word for us. That which is the authentic existence is just a word for us, but what is only an appearance we take to be truth.

The soul is not known to us, but the body is daily seen by us. What is daily seen becomes truth for us. That is why I have said that the body is death-oriented and is itself a death. The soul is immortal, not death-oriented. But upon its deathlessness there is the dance of death of the body.

We have no difficulty in understanding the sea and the wave because we have not seen any enmity between them. But immortality and death are difficult to understand because we have assumed them to be enemies; that is our belief. When I talk about the sea and the wave, their existences are closely linked, so there does not seem to be any opposition. But immortality and death appear as stark enemies – as opposites. It seems they can never be one. But they are also one. The more closely and deeply you know death, the more you will find that death is nothing more than change.

The wave is also a change. The deeper you search into immortality, the more you will find it is nothing more than eternity. The existence of whatsoever appears to be in opposition in this world is based upon its opposite. Our difficulty is that it appears to us as opposite. We maintain a separation between death and immortality – but death cannot survive without the deathless. For death to exist, it has to seek the support of that which is deathless. As long as death is there, it needs the support of that which is immortal.

Even for a lie to exist, it can do so only with the support of truth. For a lie to exist, it also has to claim that it is truth. Truth never claims to be truth, but the lie always claims that it is truth. It cannot travel an inch without such a claim. It has to vociferously announce, "Be careful; I am coming. I am truth." It carries many certificates with it to prove why it is truth.

Truth needs no certificate; it needs no support from lies. If truth takes their support, it will be in difficulty. If the lie does not take the support of truth, then the lie will be in difficulty.

For immortality, the support of death is not necessary, but it is only in relation to the concept of immortality that the occurrence of death is understood. The pure existence has no need for that which is changeable, but what is changing can be understood only in relation to that which is changeless. One thing is certain, that we understand only the changeable – because that is what we are. That is why, whenever we think about immortality, we try to understand it only through that which is changeable. There is no other way.

Our condition is like one who is in darkness trying to guess what light is. He has no other way. Darkness is only a very dim form of light. It is a condition of the minimum possible light. Where there is no light at all, there is no such thing as darkness. Light may be or it may be beyond the power of our eyes to grasp it.

Our senses grasp things only within certain limits. Otherwise, the beams of highly intense light that constantly pass by us would make us instantly blind if we were to see them. As long as we did not know what the x-ray was we did not know that the rays of the x-ray could pass through a human body. We did not know that a picture of our inside bones could be taken from outside. If not today, then tomorrow we may be able to find a ray which can penetrate through the initial cell of a newly conceived child in its mother's womb and enable us to see what will be the entire lifespan of that child after its birth. And there is a possibility of this happening.

Many types of rays pass by us, but our eyes cannot catch them. What we are calling darkness is simply light which our eyes are not capable of seeing. Because our eyes cannot see certain light rays, for us they appear to be nothing more than darkness. What we call darkness is just that light which our eyes cannot see. Therefore, any inferences a person standing in darkness makes about light are likely to be wrong, as darkness is only a form, a shade of light. Although death is only a change in the form of immortality, any inferences drawn about immortality from one viewing death would also be wrong. If we know what immortality is, only then does something happen; otherwise not.

People surrounded by death only understand immortality to mean that we will not die. But they are wrong. One who knows what immortality is knows that he was never there at all. The difference is very deep and fundamental. A person seeing death thinks that if it is true that the soul is immortal he will not die. His thinking is future-oriented. He is living in the future and is worried about it, so his understanding will be future-oriented. But one who knows what immortality is would say, "I am not there at all; I was never born." He will be past-oriented.

Because all scientific knowledge is surrounded by death, science always talks about the future. And since the whole of religion is surrounded by immortality, it always talks about the past – about the origin, not about the end. It is concerned with the basic source. Religion talks about from where the world has come, from where we have come. Religion says that if we know completely from where we have come – our source and our beginning – we will not be worried about where we will go, because we cannot go anywhere but back toward that source. Our origin is our destiny, our search, our end.

Religious thinking is concerned with the search for the origin – with what is the origin. From where has this world come? From where has this existence, this soul, this world, come? Religious thinking is in search for the past, for our origins. All sciences are in a future-oriented search – for where we are going, where we will reach, what we will become, what will happen tomorrow, what the end is. The search of science is conducted by those who are death-oriented. Religious thinking is done by those for whom death has ceased to have any meaning.

It is interesting to note that death is always in the future. Death has nothing to do with the past. Whenever you are thinking about death, the past is of no consequence, of no importance. Death lies in the tomorrow, but the source from where life has come is always in yesterday. From where life is coming, from where the

Ganges is flowing, is the source, Gangotri. But where the Ganges will empty itself is the sea. It began in the yesterday and will end in the tomorrow.

Thus a person surrounded by death will always draw conclusions that are colored by death. What is factual about a higher plane can only be guesswork on the part of the lower plane. The facts of the second plane should be evaluated by the experiences of the second plane only. It is, therefore, interesting to note that one who knows the second plane naturally knows the first plane too, but one who knows the first does not necessarily know the second. That is why, if we have described Buddha, Krishna and Christ as highly intelligent and wise, it is due to a special reason: they know all the planes; we know only one. That is why what they say is more meaningful. And whatsoever we know, they surely know. There is no difficulty in this. They have known death; they have also known misery, anger and violence. Theirs is the experience of all the planes.

In Western countries all knowledge is just accumulation on the same plane. Whatever Einstein might have been knowing, the difference between his knowledge and ours is merely quantitative. For example, we can only measure this table, but he can measure the whole world. This difference is of quantity or of degree. There is no qualitative difference. This means that he does not know something which is different from what you may know, but what he knows is just an extension in quantity of what may be known to you. You may know less, he knows more. You have only one dollar, he may have a million. But your dollar and his million are not qualitatively different. What he has is not different from what you have.

When we call Buddha or Mahavira *gyanis,* knowers, what we mean is different. It is possible that on our plane we may know more than they know, but our calling them gyanis means that they know something of another plane about which we do not know anything. They have gone into a new dimension which has a qualitative difference.

If Mahavira and Einstein should encounter each other, it may even happen that Mahavira will not prove to be a knower of things that are known to Einstein. He may not have as much accumulation of knowledge as Einstein. Mahavira may say, "I can only measure a table; you are able to measure the whole earth. You can even tell the distance of the moon and the stars from the earth; I cannot do that. If I can measure this room even, it is enough for me. But still, I would say that you are not more learned or knowledgeable than me because you only know that which is ordinarily plausible."

If a room can be measured, the stars can also be measured. There is no transcendence in doing so. Within Einstein there is no mutation or change; he is not a different man. He remains the same person, though he is more efficient where we are inefficient. It is only that he has a much greater speed on the same plane, while we are very slow. Einstein has traveled far on the same plane where we have traveled very little. Einstein went deep where others only touched the periphery, but Einstein has not moved into another plane.

When we call Buddha or Mahavira or others of their category knowers, we mean that they have gone beyond the plane of death to where they have known immortality, and what they tell us about this is invaluable. We may understand it this way: if a person who has never drunk any alcohol makes a statement about it, the statement has no value. If a person who has drunk alcohol makes a statement about it, then also it has no value. But the statements of a person who has drunk alcohol and who has gone beyond it have value.

One who has not drunk alcohol at all is a child. His statements will be childish. That is why people who have never drunk any alcohol have not been able to understand those who drink. Those who drink say, "We have known what you know, but now we know something more." If you drink, then you can say something about it. But those who have drunk themselves full and who have then left it have something more to say. Alcoholics will listen to them.

In Europe and America, there are societies of ex-alcoholics. Alcoholics Anonymous is a widespread institution. Only those who have once been alcoholic can become members of this institution, and this movement was started in order to enable other alcoholics to give up drinking. What is surprising is that such associations of alcoholics can make others who are alcoholics give up drinking very quickly, because what such alcoholics say comes from their maturity. Their statements are understood better by the drinkers because what they are telling is from experience. They also have drunk and faltered and fallen flat repeatedly, and have passed through all the experiences of the drunkard. That is why their statements, which come out of experience, have a value.

But this I have told only by way of an illustration. Whether you drink or do not drink or give up drinking, there is no difference in the plane you are on. You are still on the same plane. The difference is only that of different rungs on the same ladder. But once you experience deathlessness, there is a change of plane. The great impact of the teachings of Buddha, Mahavira and Christ is due to the fact that although they knew that which we ordinarily know, they also knew something beyond what we know. From the new knowledge that they had, they could say that there were fundamental errors in our knowing.

*While discussing Mahavira,
You had said that Mahavira had achieved
total self-realization in his previous birth
and that he took another birth out of compassion only
in order to express and tell to others what he had seen
and known. Similarly, You said that Krishna was fully
enlightened from his very birth.
Previously, when I had a discussion with You in
Jabalpur, I had an intuition that what You had said
about Mahavira and Krishna is also applicable to You.
Is it true then that You also took birth out of*

> *compassion? In this context, would You kindly throw light on Your previous births and Your achievements in them so that it may be useful to seekers? Please also explain what was the time gap between Your last birth and this one.*

IN this connection, many things will have to be kept in mind. Firstly, in connection with the birth of people like Krishna, it should be understood that when their attainment of self-realization is completed in a particular life, it is entirely their freedom to choose whether to take another birth or not. It is a fact that if they take birth, that birth is taken with full freedom of choice.

No birth prior to attainment of self-realization is taken out of freedom. One has no choice in other births. Other births are due to the compulsions of our desires — as if we are pushed or pulled into a birth by our past actions and pulled forward by our desires for the future. Thus, birth is ordinarily an event of helplessness.

Only in full consciousness is there an opportunity for a choice — only when one has fully known the self. That position is reached when nothing more remains to be known. Such a moment comes when one can say that "there is no future for me because for me there is no desire. There is nothing which will create any unhappiness for me if I do not get it." This condition, where for the first time you have a choice, happens when one has reached the highest peak.

It is a matter of great interest and one of the deep mysteries of life that those who desire to be free cannot be free and those who have no desire at all become free. Those who have a desire to take birth at a particular place or in a particular family have no choice but to do so. But those who have the freedom can take birth anywhere they choose, if they so desire, even though they may not exercise their choice.

A freedom of choice is there for the taking of only one more birth — not because there will not be any freedom to take still another birth, but because after one more birth the desire to use such freedom is again lost.

Freedom remains forever. In this life, if you attain the supreme experience, then you will have that freedom. But what usually happens is that after attaining this freedom, the desire for using it is not lost immediately. And this situation can be useful.

But those who have looked deeply into the matter have felt that this is also a type of bondage. This is why the Jainas, who have searched deeply in this direction – more than any other religious endeavor in this world – have described this bondage as the *teerthankara gotrabandh,* the desire to be a teacher in order to lead others towards enlightenment. This is the last bondage. It is a bondage with full freedom – the last, with only one last desire of which to make use.

It is, however, a desire. That is why there are many who have attained enlightenment, but all of them could not become teerthankaras. In order to be a teerthankara, in order to make use of this freedom, it is necessary to have a chain of a particular type of past actions. A long chain of desire to be a teacher is necessary. If this attachment for being a teacher survives, it will give the last push. Then whatever is known will be told, whatever is experienced will be described, and whatever is gained will be distributed.

After realization is attained, it is not necessary that everyone should take another birth. In such a situation, therefore, out of millions of self-realized persons, just one chooses to take one more birth. That is why the Jainas have more or less fixed an average, that in a *srishti-kalpa,* one period of creation, there can be only twenty-four teerthankaras.

It works just like any other average. For example, we say that today, on an average, so many accidents will take place on Bombay roads. The records of accidents of the last thirty years are taken into account, and an average is worked out. The forecast turns out to be more or less correct. Similarly, this happening of twenty-four teerthankaras is also an average. It is from the memory of many periods of creation that the average is worked out.

There are memories of several worlds having been born and their annihilation, and during those periods teerthankaras were born. On an average, in each such period, only about twenty-four persons are able to maintain the bond to take one more birth. In this context, it should also be remembered that when we are talking about the number of accidents on Bombay roads, we are not thinking of accidents on the roads of London, or accidents only on Marine Drive or on any one particular road of Bombay.

The calculation of the Jainas is based only upon their own path. In that calculation, the paths of Jesus, Krishna or Buddha are not taken into account. But it is also interesting to note that when Hindus tried to calculate on their path, their count of such persons was also twenty-four. Similarly, Buddhists also counted twenty-four for their path. That is why the idea of twenty-four incarnations stuck to all. The Jainas already had the idea of twenty-four teerthankaras and the Buddhists had the idea of twenty-four buddhas.

In such things, Christianity and Islam have not gone deep. But Islam did say that Mohammed was not the first such person and that there were persons like him before. Mohammed himself indicated that four persons had come before him, but the identity of those indications remained vague and incomplete. The path of Mohammed in the chain prior to him cannot be found. The path is only known to start from Mohammed himself. No one else has been able to count with the same clarity that Mahavira had in counting the twenty-four in his tradition, because with Mahavira that path was coming to an end. It is easy to be clear on past events, but Mohammed had also to think in the future, and there it is difficult to be clear.

Jesus too had tried to count people prior to him, but his calculations were vague because the road of Jesus was also new, beginning with him. Buddha also could not clearly count those prior to himself; he only made indirect references in that direction.

That is why, in the count of twenty-four buddhas, there is none prior to Buddha. In this connection, Jainas have searched deeper and are more authentic. They have kept full records of the names and addresses of those twenty-four. Thus, on every path here are twenty-four individuals. Such individuals take only one more birth after realization. That birth, I have told you, is due only to compassion.

In this world, nothing happens without a reason. The reason for taking another birth can only be one of two: either there is desire or there is compassion. There is no third reason. I can come to your house either to give something or to take something. There can be no third reason. If I come to your house to take something, it is desire. If I come to give something, it is compassion. There is no third reason or purpose for coming to your house.

All births out of desire will be dependent, because you can never be independent in a condition of craving or begging. How can a beggar be independent?

It is not possible for a beggar to be independent, because all the freedom lies with the giver. What freedom can there be for the beggar? But the giver can be free. Even if you do not take, the giver can give. But if you do not give, the beggar cannot take. It is not necessary that we take all that Mahavira and Buddha gave us, but it is certain that they have given. The taking is not certain and can be avoided, but the giving is positive and definite. The desire to distribute that which is received, realized or known is natural, but that is the last desire. Therefore, it is also called a bondage. Those who have known have described it as a bondage of action. That too is a bondage – the last bondage. So I will have to come to your house. I may come either to take or to give, but I will be bound to your house.

Even if I am not bound to your house, it makes no difference. I will have to come to your house. But there is a great difficulty: since people usually come to your house only to get something and you have also gone to others' houses only to demand something, it is naturally difficult to understand someone who comes to give you something.

I will tell you one very incomprehensible thing that happens because of this. Since you are not able to understand what it means to give, many times such individuals have had to pretend to take something from you. It will be beyond your comprehension that such compassionate people have also to consider whether to ask you for some food. That is why all of Mahavira's religious discourses were given only after having taken meals. Such discourses are just a sort of thanksgiving. It is a thanksgiving for the food that you gave.

If Mahavira should come to beg food, you immediately understand it. He will tell you a few words in return, by way of thanks, and will go away. You feel gratified that you have given two pieces of bread, an enormous task indeed! You will not be able to realize that such compassionate persons have also to consider whether you will be able to take what they wanted to give. And if there is no arrangement for you to give, your ego will find it difficult to accept.

That is why it is not without a reason that Mahavira or Buddha had to go out begging and had to demand food from you – because it will be impossible for you to tolerate a person who just goes on giving to you. You will positively become his enemy. You will find it very strange to think that you become an enemy to a person who just goes on giving to you and does not give you any opportunity to give in return. If he does not demand anything from you, a barrier is created between him and you.

That is why such a person generally asks you for small things. Sometimes he asks for meals, sometimes for clothes and sometimes he says he has no place to rest. He has taken something from you, and you become tensionless. You have become his equal, on the same level, because you have given him something more, and he has not given you anything but a few words. You have given him shelter, clothes or money. What has he given? He has only told you a few stories or given you some advice.

Buddha, therefore, called his sannyasins *bhikkhus,* and asked them to go about as beggars, because then only could they give. They would have to go about in the guise of beggars in order to create a situation in which they could easily give.

Compassion has its own problems. A person living on such a plane is facing great difficulties. We cannot understand him. He is living among people who do not understand his language and will always misunderstand him. This is unavoidable, though he is not inconvenienced or worried about it. When you misunderstand him there is no worry, because he knows that it is natural and that you are thinking and understand things from your own plane. Therefore, those realized persons who have not developed the capacity to teach in past births disappear, no sooner do they become realized; they do not take another birth.

In this connection, it is also worthwhile understanding that the taking of birth by Mahavira and Buddha in a king's family is very meaningful. Jainas had decided conclusively that a teerthankara must take birth only in a king's family. I once said that there is a story of Mahavira's soul having entered into the womb of a brahmin woman, and the Gods had to exchange the fetus with that belonging to a *kshatriya* woman, because a teerthankara had to be born only in a king's family.

Why? Because after taking birth in a king's family, if one becomes a beggar of his own free will, he will be more effective and more acceptable to people. He will be understood better by people because they have been in the habit of always taking and demanding something from their king. And because of that habit, perhaps whatever he has come to give will be taken by people.

It is our habit to always look up to a king, as he is always sitting on a higher level. Even if that king chooses to be a beggar and begs on the road, he remains on a higher level. This old habit that people have will help him. Therefore, this was a device to make it easy to give. Thus, one such as a teerthankara could be born only out of a king's family. But this was not difficult, because such a person had a choice in his hands as to where to take birth.

All those individuals like Buddha and Mahavira had attained and realized in their previous births. Then all that was attained was distributed in their last birth. It may be asked that if all this knowledge and attainment came in the previous birth, why did Mahavira and Buddha appear to make so much effort in their most recent birth to attain something?

To this question there is no answer. Due to this, confusion is created. Why should Mahavira and Buddha do so much sadhana? Krishna did not do any such thing, while Mahavira and Buddha did. This effort was not in order to attain to truth. Truth was already known to them, but to explain and express it to others is not in any way less difficult than knowing it. In fact, it is more difficult. If one has to explain certain truths, it is all the more difficult.

For example, the truth of Krishna was not in any way specialized. That is why Krishna could succeed in his efforts to give it from where he was. But the truth which Mahavira and Buddha taught happens to be very specialized. The paths which they had shown are also very peculiar. They are peculiar in this respect: for example, if Mahavira would have asked someone to go on a fast for thirty days, and if that person knew that Mahavira himself had never done any fasting, he would not be prepared to listen to Mahavira.

Mahavira had to do fasting for twelve years only for those whom he wanted to teach. Otherwise it would not have been possible to speak to them about fasting. Mahavira had to keep *mouna,* silence, for twelve years in order to convince those whom he wanted to become silent for only twelve days. Otherwise they would not listen to Mahavira.

Regarding Buddha, there is another interesting story. Buddha was starting a new meditation system whereas Mahavira was not starting a system which was new. Mahavira already had the knowledge of a fully developed science, in a tradition where he was not the first but the last. Behind him was a long chain of eminent teachers. That chain was so well preserved and secured that it was never lost. That knowledge was deposited with Mahavira as a sort of trust from the earlier teachers.

It is indeed a wonder that up until the time of Mahavira, knowledge was able to remain so continuous. Thus, Mahavira did not have to give any new truth. The truth which was to be given had been long nourished, and it had the strength of a long heritage. But Mahavira also had to create his own individuality so that people would listen to him.

It is interesting to note that the Jainas have remembered

Mahavira the most and that the earlier twenty-three teerthankaras are practically forgotten. This is surprising, as Mahavira was the last in the chain. He was neither a pioneer nor the first, nor did he have any new truth to be revealed. He revealed only those things which were already known and tested. Still, Mahavira is remembered the most, and the remaining twenty-three have become mythological.

If Mahavira had not been born, we would not have even known the names of those previous twenty-three teerthankaras. The deeper reason for this is that Mahavira spent twelve years building his image and individuality while the other teerthankaras did not. They just looked after their sadhana. Mahavira had a very well organized system. In sadhana there is no organized system, but for Mahavira, sadhana was a sort of acting which he performed very efficiently.

That is why the images of the other twenty-three teerthankaras could not emerge as clearly and as sharply as the image of Mahavira. They all appeared faint. Mahavira created his image like an accomplished artist. It was all well planned. Whatsoever he wanted to do with his personality was well prepared. He came fully prepared.

Buddha was the first in the sense that he had brought with him a new system of sadhana. Therefore, Buddha had to go through a different route. It is interesting to note that this created an illusion that Buddha went through sadhana himself. Actually, Buddha had also realized in his previous life. In this birth, he had only to distribute the harvest that he had previously reaped. But Buddha did not have an organized tradition behind him. Buddha's search was entirely his own. He carved out a new path for himself. On that same mountain where a wide highway already existed, he had carved out a new path.

Mahavira was walking on a ready-made royal path, but he had to announce it again because people very often tend to forget such things. But the path was already there for him. Buddha had to break new ground, so he made a different type of arrangement in his life. First he went through all sorts of sadhanas. And after passing through each such sadhana, he said that it was useless and that no one could reach anywhere through it. In the end he announced his own method, saying that he had reached that way and that anyone could reach that way.

This was, one may say, very much a prearranged affair – very well arranged! He who wants to introduce a new practice will have to declare that all old practices are false. And if Buddha would have called them false without passing through them, as Krishnamurti does, then the effect would not have been any more than the effect of what Krishnamurti tells, because one does not have a right to declare anything which is not within one's experience as false.

Recently, someone who comes to me had also gone to see Krishnamurti and had asked him about *kundalini*. Krishnamurti had said that it is all useless. Then, to the person who reported this I asked whether he has asked this from experience – whether he asked it after experimenting with kundalini – or without doing so. If it was asked without experimenting or passing through it, then it was useless. If it was asked after experimenting, then another question should be asked to him: whether he was successful or whether he was unsuccessful.

If he was successful, then it was wrong to say it is useless. If he was unsuccessful, it does not necessarily follow that others also are bound to be unsuccessful in experimenting. Therefore, Buddha had to pass through all practices and had to show that this practice was wrong or that one was wrong and that no one would reach anywhere through it. Then he could say, "I have reached by this method, and I am telling you from experience."

Mahavira passed through all the same practices, but he announced that they had been practiced for ages and were useful. Buddha had said that everything was useless, and he opened up a new direction. But both of them had realized in their previous birth.

Krishna also had realized in his previous birth, but Krishna did not introduce any new special technique for self-realization. Krishna indicated a particular way to live life. Therefore, there was no need of passing through any process of meditation or austerity, because that itself would be an obstacle.

If Mahavira had said that it is possible to attain *moksha* even while sitting in your own shop, then Mahavira's own effort in developing his individuality would have seemed futile. Then people would ask Mahavira, "Why did you give up everything then?" If Krishna had gone into a forest to meditate and then stood on the battlefield and said that even on the battlefield one can attain, no one would have listened to him. Then Arjuna also would have asked him why he wanted to deceive him. If Krishna himself would have gone to the forest, why should he prevent Arjuna from doing so?

So it depends upon every teacher how and what he wants to give. Then an appropriate effort, a living endeavor, has to be made in that context. Often he will have to make arrangements in life that are totally artificial. But this is unavoidable for what he wants to give.

Now this question which you have asked about me is a little difficult to answer. It is easier for me to reply if asked about Mahavira or Buddha or Krishna. But still, two or three things can be kept in view. Firstly, my previous birth took place about seven hundred years ago. More difficulties are there due to that fact.

Mahavira's previous birth was about two hundred and fifty years before his birth as Mahavira. Buddha's previous birth was only seventy-eight years before his birth as Buddha. In Buddha's case, there were even people living who could stand witness to the fact of his previous birth. Even during the lifetime of Mahavira, there were people who could remember having met Mahavira in their previous birth. Krishna's birth as Krishna was about two thousand years after his last birth, and so all the names of enlightened *rishis* that Krishna had given were very ancient. It was not even possible to remember them historically.

Seven hundred years is a very long period. But for the one who is taking birth after seven hundred years it is not very long, because when one is not in the body there is no difference between one moment and seven hundred years. Time measurement begins only with the body. Outside the body, it makes no difference whether you have been for seven hundred years or seven thousand years. Only upon acquiring a body does the difference begin.

It is also very interesting to note the method for knowing the time interval between the last death and the current birth. Speaking about myself, how did I come to know that I was not here for seven hundred years? It is very difficult to just figure it out directly. I can only judge or calculate the time by observing those people who took several births during this time interval.

Suppose, for example, that a particular person was known to me during my lifetime seven hundred years ago. In between for me there was a gap, but he may have taken birth ten times. However, there are memories of his past ten births. From his memories only can I calculate how long I must have remained without a body. Otherwise it is difficult to calculate and determine this, because our time scale and methods of measurement do not belong to the time that prevails beyond body or in the bodiless state. Our measurements of time are in the world of bodily existence.

It is something like this, that for a moment I go to sleep and see a dream. In the dream I see that years have passed, and after some moments you awaken me and say that I had been dozing. I ask you how much time has been passed in dozing, and you reply, "It was not even for a moment." I say, "How is that possible? I have seen a dream sequence of several years."

In a dream, an expanse of several years can be seen within a moment. The time scale of dream life is different. If, after awakening from a dream, the dreamer had no way of knowing when he went to sleep, then it would be difficult to determine the length of his sleep. That can be known only by a clock. For example, when I was previously awake it was twelve o'clock, and now that I have woken up after sleeping it is only one minute past twelve. Otherwise I can only know because you were here also; there is no other way of knowing. So only in this way has it been determined that seven hundred years have passed.

And another thing you have asked me is whether I was born with full realization. Concerning this, there are a few things to be understood which are important.

It can be said that I was born with *nearabout* full knowledge. I say nearabout only because some steps have been left out deliberately, and deliberately that can be done.

In this connection also, the Jaina thinking is very scientific. They have divided knowledge into fourteen steps. Thirteen steps are in this world and the fourteenth is in the beyond. Out of these *gunasthana* – these first thirteen steps – some of them are such that they could be left out; they are optional. It is not necessary that one should pass through all of them. Such layers can all be passed through also, but one who jumps over them can never keep the *teerthankara bandh* intact.

Whatsoever is optional must also be known by the teacher. Optional subjects must also be studied by the teacher. For the student, whatsoever must be known in order to get through an examination is sufficient. But the teacher has to understand everything, even what is optional.

In these thirteen steps of self-realization, there are a few things that are optional. There are certain dimensions of realization about which it is not necessary to know in order to become enlightened. One can go straight to moksha. But for one to be a teacher, those dimensions must also be known.

Another important thing to be noted is that after a certain stage of development, for example, after the attainment of twelve steps, the length of time that it takes to achieve the remaining steps can be stretched out. They can be attained either in one birth, two births or in three births. Great use can be made of postponement.

As I said previously, after the attainment of full realization there is no further possibility of taking birth more than one time more. Such an enlightened one is not likely to cooperate or be helpful for more than one additional birth. But after reaching twelve steps, if two can be set aside, then such a person can be useful for many births more. And the possibility is there to set them aside.

On reaching the twelfth step, the journey has nearabout come to an end. I say nearabout: that means that all walls have collapsed; only a transparent curtain remains through which everything can be seen. However the curtain is there. After lifting it, there is no difficulty in going beyond. After going beyond the curtain, whatsoever you are ordinarily able to see can be seen from the other side of the curtain also. There is no difference at all.

So this is why I say nearabout: by taking one step more, one can go beyond the curtain. But then there is a possibility of only one more birth, while if one remains on this side of the curtain one can take as many births as one wants. After crossing into the beyond, there is no way of coming back more than once to this side of the curtain.

One might ask whether Mahavira and Buddha knew this. Yes, this was clear to them, and it could have been utilized by them also. But there are fundamental differences of circumstances.

It is of interest to note that after attaining full self-realization, that realization can only be taught to very advanced students, not to all. For those people on whom Buddha and Mahavira were working during their several births, for those who were walking beside them in many forms, for them, one more birth was just sufficient. Sometimes it so happened that even one more birth was not necessary. If in one's present life one attained realization at the age of twenty, and if one is to live until age sixty, then if he can complete the work in the remaining forty years, the matter ends; there is no necessity to come back.

But now the situation is very strange. Those who can be called developed sadhaks are as good as nil. In order to work on such sadhaks, future teachers will have to work for many births. Then only can the work be completed; not otherwise.

For Mahavira or Buddha the situation was different because when they were about to leave the last life they could find a few people around them to whom further work could be entrusted. That situation does not exist now.

Today, man is totally an extrovert. That is why today the teacher has difficulties such as were not there previously. Not only does he have to work harder with a greater number of undeveloped people, but there is also the fear that his labor may go to waste.

Again, it is not possible to find suitable individuals to whom further work can be entrusted. This happened in the case of Guru Nanak of the Sikh tradition.

Up to Gobind Singh, up to the tenth Sikh guru, it was possible to find the next man. But Gobind Singh had to stop that practice. Gobind Singh tried very hard, such as none had done before him, to find the eleventh man for keeping the chain intact. But he could not find anyone. He had to close the search, and there ended the chain. Now there can be no eleventh man because it can happen only in close continuity. Once there is the slightest break or gap, it is not possible to pass on what is to be transferred.

Bodhidharma, a realized disciple of Buddha, had to go from India to China, because in China there was a person to whom it was possible to transfer his knowledge. The Buddhist tradition itself moved out of India as a consequence. People understood from this that a few Buddhist monks went to China in order to spread Buddhism, but this notion is wrong. This is the understanding of those who see the events of history superficially.

Hui-Ke was the name of a person in China to whom it was possible to transfer knowledge, and it is interesting to note that he was not willing to come to India. The difficulties of this world are often very surprising. Hui-Ke was not willing to come because he was not aware of his potential. Therefore, Bodhidharma had to go on a long journey all the way to China. Then again a time came when the secrets of the Buddhist tradition had to be shifted to Japan, for the same transfer of knowledge.

This gap of seven hundred years was a period of several difficulties for me. The difficulties were these: Firstly, it was becoming more and more difficult to take birth. For any person who reaches a certain stage of development, it is difficult to find suitable parents for another birth. During the time of Mahavira and Buddha there was no such difficulty. Daily, wombs were available through which such advanced souls could take birth.

In the time of Mahavira, there were eight fully realized persons in Bihar – all of the same level as Mahavira. They were working from eight different ways. The nearabout condition was reached by thousands. There were not a few, but thousands to whom the work could be entrusted for proper care and further transmission.

Nowadays, if someone of that high level wants to take birth, he may have to wait for a few thousand years. Another difficulty is that during the interval the work he may have done could get lost. In between, the individuals on whom he may have done some work would have taken ten more births, and it would be difficult to cut through the layers upon layers of those ten births.

Nowadays, any master will have to pass through a much longer period before finally lifting the curtain and going beyond. He will have to hold himself back. Once he goes beyond the curtain, he will not be ready or willing to take another birth. He will still have a choice of whether or not to take one more birth, but he will think it to be futile. There is a reason for this. He can take one more birth, but for whom? In one birth, it is not possible to achieve much.

If I know that by coming into this room I can complete my work within an hour, then it is worth coming. If the work cannot be done, it is not useful to come. In this respect, compassion has a twofold purpose. First, it wants to give something to you; second, it knows also that if it only takes something away from you and is not able to give as well, then you will be in great danger. Your difficulties will not decrease but will increase. If I am able to show you something, it is well and good. But if I am not able to show you and you become blind to whatever you were previously able to see, then the situation is worse.

In connection with these seven hundred years, a few other things may also be noted. First, I did not have any idea that such a talk would ever arise. Some time back, suddenly in Poona this matter came up. My mother had come. She was asked by Ramlal Pungalia whether she remembered some very early peculiar incident about me and if she would kindly relate it to him.

I was under the impression that there was no possibility of such a matter ever coming up. I also did not know when they talked with each other. Recently, he declared this in a meeting, that my mother had told him that I did not weep for three days after birth, and I did not take any milk for three days. This was her first remembrance about me.

This is true. Seven hundred years ago, in my previous life, there was a spiritual practice of twenty-one days, to be done before death. I was to give up my body after a total fast of twenty-one days. There were reasons for this, but I could not complete those twenty-one days. Three days remained. Those three days I had to complete in this life. This life is a continuation from there. The intervening period does not have any meaning in this respect. When only three days remained in that life, I was killed. Twenty-one days could not be completed because I was killed just three days before, and those three days were omitted.

In this life, those three days were completed. If those twenty-one days could have been completed in that life, then perhaps it would not have been possible to take more than one birth. Now in this context, many things are worth noting.

Standing in front of that curtain and not crossing over is very difficult. Seeing that curtain and still not to lift it is very difficult. It is difficult constantly to remain aware of the matter of when the curtain will be lifted. It is very nearly an impossible task to stand in front of that curtain and still not lift it. But this could happen only because three days before the completion of the fast, I was killed.

Therefore, I have told many times in various discussions that just as Judas tried for a long time to kill Jesus, though Judas had no enmity with Jesus, the person who killed me had no enmity with me, though he was taken to be, and was treated as, an enemy.

That killing became valuable. At the time of death, those three days were left. After all my strenuous effort for enlightenment during that life, I was able to achieve in this life, after a period of twenty-one years, that which had been possible to achieve during those three days. For each of those three days in that life, I had to spend seven years in this life. That is why I say that from my last life alone I have not come with full realization. I say instead that I have come with nearabout complete realization. The curtain could have been lifted, but then there could be only one birth more.

Now I can take still another birth. There is now a possibility of one more birth. But that will depend on whether I feel that it will be useful. During this whole life I shall go on striving to see whether one more birth will be of some use. Then it is worthwhile taking birth; otherwise the matter is over and it is no use making any more effort. So that killing was valuable and useful.

As I have told you, time measurement while in the body is different from the calculation of time in other states of consciousness. At the time of birth, time is moving very slowly. At the time of death, time is moving very rapidly. We have not understood the speed of time because in our understanding time has no speed. We understand only that in time all things move.

Up until now, even the most eminent scientists did not have any idea that time also has a velocity. The reason for this is that if we fix or decide the velocity of time, then it will be difficult to measure all other velocities. Therefore, we have kept time steady. We say that in one hour someone has walked three miles. But if within three miles the hour also walks somewhat, it will create many difficulties. We have, therefore, made the hour steady and static; otherwise everything would be in confusion. Thus, we have made time static. But the most interesting fact is that time is non-static, and it is more fickle and moves more than anything else. Time means change. We have kept that fixed, hammered in like a tent peg. It is done precisely for the reason that without its being fixed, measurement of all other movements will be impossible. This time-velocity also runs more or less in accordance with one's state of mind.

The time-velocity of a child is slow, but that of an old man is very fast, compact and contracted. In a short span, time moves very fast for old people, whereas for a child time moves very slowly, in a large span. For every animal also, time moves differently. A human child takes fourteen years to grow only as much as a puppy grows in a few months. The offspring of some animals grow still faster.

Some animals are born almost full size. The moment they put their feet on the ground, there is no difference between them and the adults of their species. They are complete. That is why animals do not have much sense of time. Movement is very fast for them. It is so fast that no sooner does the colt put its feet on the ground than it walks. It cannot conceive that there is a time gap between being born and being able to walk.

The human child can conceive of that time gap, and so man is an animal troubled by time. He is, so to speak, always in tension, racing against time as it is continuously passing and running on, keeping him lagging behind.

In the last moments of my previous life, the remaining work could have been done in only three days because time was very compact. My age was one hundred and six years. Time was moving very fast. The story of those three days continued in my childhood of this birth. In my previous life it was at its end, but to finish that work here in this life took twenty-one years.

Many a time, if the opportunity is missed, it may be necessary to spend as many as seven years for every single day. So in this life I did not come with full realization, but came with nearabout full realization. But now I will have to make my arrangements differently.

As I told you, Mahavira had to contrive a tapascharya, a system of austerities, through which he could give. Buddha had to contrive still other methods to falsify all austerities – one after the other. This was also a type of austerity. What Mahavira and Buddha did not have to do, I have to do. Just for nothing, I have to read everything that there is in the world. It is all useless; I have no use for it. But to the modern world, which does not bother about the one who goes on a fast or the one who sits with his eyes closed, no message can be given through practicing austerities. If anyone can be reached by any austerity, it is only through that of my having digested the great accumulation of intellectual knowledge that is daily growing bigger and bigger.

That is why I have spent my whole life with books. I would say that Mahavira was not troubled much by remaining on a fast, but I have had to take the trouble of reading so much that is of no use to me. However, only after taking that trouble can I communicate and make my message intelligible to this world; otherwise not. The modern age of science can understand only in its own language.

If these things become clear to you, it is not difficult for you also to start having some idea about your previous births. I wish that I can soon make you remember such things, because if you can remember it will save a lot of time and energy. Ordinarily, it so happens that you start your life not from where you had left off in the previous one, but in every birth you start again from almost ABC. If you can remember your past, then you do not have to start from ABC, but you can start from where you had left off. And then only is it possible to make progress, not otherwise.

Now this is worth understanding: Animals have not been progressing at all. Scientists are puzzled that animals have been reproducing themselves without further evolution. The monkey has only a slightly less developed brain than a man, but the evolutionary difference is much greater than the difference in brain. What is the matter? What could be the difficulty? Why are the monkeys not coming out of this repetitive circle? They are right there where they were a million years ago.

We are thinking that the evolutionary process is going on everywhere, but it is all very uncertain. Darwin's hypothesis is very confusing because for hundreds and thousands of years monkeys are where they have always been; they are not developing. A squirrel remains a squirrel and does not develop. The cow remains a cow without further development. So development is not automatic; there is something else that is creating the difference.

Every monkey has to start from where his father started. The son cannot start from where the father had ended. The father is not able to communicate; he is not able to make his son start from where he left off during his life. How can there be any progress? Each time a son begins from the same point.

Similar is the condition regarding the development of the soul. If you are starting this life from where you had started in the previous life, you cannot develop. In a spiritual sense, there will be no evolution for you. In every birth you will start from the same point where you had started previously. If the starting point remains the same, then there is no evolution.

Evolution or development means that the previous ending point should be the starting point; otherwise there will be no evolution. Man could make progress because he has invented a language for communication. What the father knows he can teach his child. Education means this, that that which the generation of the father has come to know can be handed down to the generation of the son.

But the son will not have to start from where the father had started. If the son can start from where the father has left off, then there will be progress. Then the movement will not be in the form of a circle, but in the form of a spiral. Then the child will not move in a circle, but will begin climbing. He will begin climbing as if he were on a hill. What is true for the general human evolution is also true for the spiritual evolution of an individual.

If you do not have any communication between this life and the previous one, then you have not inquired at all into your previous life. You have not inquired into where you have left off so that you could begin from there. Because of this it may be that you will again erect the same edifice from its foundation which you had already constructed in the last life. Again you will lay the foundation. If you go on only laying the foundation, then when will you complete the construction of the building?

Therefore, what little I have told you about my previous life is not because it has any value or that you may know something about me. I have told you this only because it may make you reflect about yourselves and set you in search of your past lives. The moment you know your past lives, there will be a spiritual revolution and evolution. Then you will start from where you had left off in your last life; otherwise you will get lost in endless lives and reach nowhere. There will only be a repetition.

There has to be a link, a communication, between this life and the previous one. Whatsoever you had achieved in your previous life should come to be known, and you should have the capacity to take the next step forwards. That is why Buddha and Mahavira discussed the matter of previous lives in great detail. This was not done by earlier teachers.

The teachers of the Vedas and the Upanishads had told everything about supreme knowledge, but they did not connect it with the science of knowing about previous births. By the time Mahavira took birth, the need for this became clear. It was clear that it was not sufficient only to tell what you can become. It was necessary also to tell what you have been, because without the support and help of what you have been, your potentialities cannot blossom, you cannot become that which you *can* become.

This is why a full forty years in the lives of Mahavira and Buddha were spent in trying to make people remember their previous births. As long as a person did not remember his last life, he was told that he need not bother about his further progress. He should first see clearly his road and the point up to which he had reached, then take a further step. Otherwise there would only be a running forwards and backwards on the same road again and again to no avail. That is why the remembering of previous births became an absolutely unavoidable first step.

Nowadays the difficulty is this: it is not very difficult to make you remember your previous births, but the thing called courage has been lost. It is possible to make you remember your previous births only if you have achieved the capacity to remain undisturbed in the midst of the very difficult memories of this life. Otherwise it is not possible.

Memories of this birth are not so difficult to take, but when the memories of previous births break upon you, it will be very difficult. While the memories of this life come in installments, those of previous lives break upon you in their entirety.

In this life, what we suffer today is forgotten the next day and what we suffer the next day is forgotten the day after. But the memories of your previous lives will break upon you in their entirety, not in fragments. Will you be able to bear it? You gain the capacity to bear the memories of past lives only when you are able to bear the worst conditions of life. Whatsoever happens, nothing should make a difference to you.

When no memory of this life can be a cause of anxiety to you, only then can you be led into the memories of past lives. Otherwise those memories may become great traumas for you, and the door to such traumas cannot be opened unless you have the capacity and worthiness to face them.

3

PATHS ARE MANY
THE TRAVELERS ARE FEW

March 10, 1971

*Does the ritual of twenty-one days which You indicated
You were doing in Your previous birth belong to any
particular tradition of meditation and self-experience?
Because from Your speeches, it appears
that You are definitely representing the methods
of some great teacher or teerthankara.
In view of this, may I also dare to ask whether You wish
to connect a spiritual link to some traditional chain, or
like Buddha are You attempting to cut a new path on
some mountain?*

TRADITIONAL thinking will remain traditional, and Buddha's path is also not new now. What has long been walked upon has become an old path, but new paths paved after the breaking of old traditions are also not new. Upon them also many persons have traveled.

Buddha had cut a new path; Mahavira walked upon an established path. But in the chain of Mahavira also, there was a first man who had cut a new path. Mahavira's path was also not the oldest. The first teerthankara had done the same type of work as Buddha. It is not a new thing to cut a new path; otherwise traditions would never be born. Now, in the context of the present situation, it is necessary to do something different than both of these things, because nowadays people of both these types are in abundance.

If we look at George Gurdjieff, he was reestablishing an old tradition like Mahavira. If we look at J. Krishnamurti, he appears to be establishing a new tradition like Buddha. But both of these are old patterns.

Many traditions are broken and many are made anew. That tradition which is new today will become old tomorrow. The situation of today is such that neither Mahavira nor Buddha could have an enduring appeal, because people are weary of that which is old. A new situation has been created in which people are growing weary even of that which is new. The new was always thought to be the opposite of the old, but now we are standing at a point from where it can be clearly seen that the new is only the beginning of the old. The new means that which will become old. No sooner do we begin explaining something as new when the thing begins to become old. Now there is no attraction to the new, and we have always had a revulsion for the old.

There was a time when there was an attraction for the old. This attraction was deep. The older a thing, the more valuable it was thought to be. If it had passed through experience, if it was well examined, there was no fear in following it, and one had full faith in it. So many people had walked on such an old path and so many had reached by that path, that new travelers could even walk with closed eyes if they wanted to. There was a road for the blind also. There was no need for anyone to doubt very much, think very much, search very much or decide very much.

And it is very difficult to decide about the unknown. However much you may doubt, in the end the jump into the unknown is only through trust, because doubt can, at the most, take you up to the point of some trust through which in the end you can jump. But that attraction for antiquity is lost, and it has become lost for several reasons.

The first reason is this, that when a person knew only one

tradition, there was no difficulty. But when one person came to know about several traditions, difficulties arose. There was a time when a Hindu born into a Hindu family was brought up solely in Hindu surroundings and near a Hindu temple. The sound of the bells of the Hindu temple had become associated with the mother's milk and had become part of his bloodstream. Thus, the presiding deity in the temple was as much a part of his bones, blood and flesh as were the air, the water and the nearby mountain.

There were no rivals. There was no church, no mosque. No sound of any other tradition fell into his ears and mind. The old was so much in existence that it could not be questioned. It had existed long before him, and he grew up with it and within it. But then, slowly, a mosque came up near the temple and a church and a *gurudwara* also followed.

At one time, tradition had an impact on everyone, but now confusion is natural. Nothing can be accepted without suspicion because opposing thoughts exist side by side. If the temple is calling you by its ringing bells, the nearby call for prayers from a mosque simultaneously tells you not to make the mistake of going to the temple. Then both of these concepts enter the mind simultaneously.

The basic reason for the increase in skepticism in the world is not an increase in man's intelligence. Man is only as intelligent as he ever was. The main reason for the increase in skepticism is the superimposition of the impressions of many traditions at once upon his intellect – particularly those of contradictory cultures.

Every path will call the other wrong. This is due to helplessness. It is not because the other path is actually wrong. Nevertheless, it will have to be called wrong, because if the other path cannot be called wrong, then the strength behind calling one's own path right is broken. In fact, if one claims that he is right, it invariably follows that the other is wrong.

Every tradition, therefore, had its own path. These paths never met or crossed each other but simply ran parallel; all traditions flowed separately in their own course. In that situation, in that period of time, the ancient had a very deep attraction, and a person like Mahavira was very useful and helpful. But as the traditions increased in number and grew in their rivalry, the old became ambiguous and the new increased in value. The new made rival claims also. But when the old traditions were only confusing the mind more and more and the arguments of the rivals could not settle anything, then instead of selecting from the old it was easier to select from the new.

There are many reasons for new traditions. First, the prophets and teerthankaras of older traditions were born thousands of years ago. Thus, their voices have become very feeble. The prophet of a new tradition is existing with you, so his voice becomes deep and powerful. The older tradition speaks in an old language that existed at the time when it was born. A new teerthankara or buddha speaks a new language that is currently being shaped. The old words and phrases that have become dubious are dropped. New words are coined which are, in a sense, virgin, and one can easily depend on them.

Thus, the attraction for the new slowly increased just as several traditions came in close contact and met. We began to live, so to speak, at a crossroads, a junction where all roads met or ended.

But now there is no attraction for the new either, because now we have come to know that all that is new becomes old in the end, and whatsoever is old was once new. We also know now that the difference between the old and the new is only of words. It is only that the new is moving faster. Within approximately three hundred years, the new acquired the same reputation and status that the old once had.

At one time the antiquity of something was a certificate of its rightness. Nowadays, newness in itself has become the proof of something being right. To prove that something is new is enough for people to begin to trust in it, just as in the past they trusted in all that was ancient. Nowadays, to call something old is in itself a condemnation.

So all traditions became busy making themselves new. Every

tradition developed propounders who talked about the new. The old paths remained, and the new ones also were found to have people walking upon them. But when this attraction for the new became strong, one unique phenomenon took place.

At the time when the antiquity of a tradition was taken as the proof of its being right, all religions were trying to prove that theirs was the oldest and the most ancient. If one asked the Jainas they would say that theirs was the most ancient tradition and that even the Vedas were born afterwards. If one asked the Vedantists, they would say that the Vedas were the oldest, and they would try to trace their origin as far back as possible – because the more ancient, the higher the status.

Similarly, when newness became the status symbol, the question arose, "How new?" About fifty years ago in America, where the attraction for the new was the strongest due to the fact that American civilization and society were the most new, there were two generations – one of the old people and the other of the younger people.

But now a very strange thing has happened. At present in America there are not only two generations. Today there is a separate generation of forty-year-olds, a separate generation of thirty-year-olds, and again a separate one for twenty- and fifteen-year-olds. The thirty-year-olds say, "Do not trust those who are over thirty years old." And even twenty-five-year-olds are now useless. High school students are now taking twenty-five-year-old collegians to be old. It has never happened before that there could be so many generations in a span of fifty years. No one even imagined that there could be grades even in the generation of young people, and that the twenty-year-olds would label the twenty-five-year-olds out of date and as good as dead.

So when innovation moves at such a rapid pace, the attraction for the new also becomes lost, because no sooner is the attraction for the new established than it becomes old. It takes time even to become attracted. A religion is not like a new fad or a new style of clothes that can be changed every six months. Nor is religion like the seed of some seasonal flower that can be uprooted four months after it has been sown. A religion is very much like a banyan tree: it takes a few thousand years to grow to full stature. And if the trees are to be changed every four or five years, then they will not be banyan trees; they can only be like seasonal-flower trees.

So the attraction for the new is also becoming lost. I have told all this only to make it clear that my way is of a third type. Neither do I believe that Mahavira's language of antiquity would be effective, nor do I think that a proclamation in favor of the new can be of any consequence. Both are outmoded. I feel that now an emphasis on that which is eternal is meaningful. That which is always is what is meaningful – neither the old nor the new.

Eternal means that which is neither old nor new. The old and the new are both only events in time, and religion has suffered on account of both. Religion has suffered at the hands of the old and the same has happened in its association with the new.

Krishnamurti is still insisting upon the new. The reason is that his grasp on events goes back to the period between 1915 and 1920 when there was much attraction for the new in this world. At that time, the new was still influential. Even now he still continues to propagate it.

Now, on this earth, there is only one possibility. All traditions have come so close to each other that if one tradition says that it alone is the only right one it would immediately create a doubt. There was a time when if a tradition claimed that it was right and impartial and true in an absolute sense, one was able to trust it. Now such a claim would only create distrust; such a claim would only be a symptom of madness. It would prove that the claimant is not a very intelligent man, that he is not a deep thinker, and that he is dogmatic and fanatical.

Bertrand Russell has written somewhere that he has never seen an intelligent person speaking in absolute terms. Those who are intelligent will definitely hesitate to assert themselves in this way. Only the foolish can be so assertive. Russell is trying to say that only the ignorant can claim anything to be the absolute truth.

As knowledge increases, such absolute announcements cannot be made. In this age, if anyone tries to assert that one particular tradition is the only right one, he will harm that tradition very much. Similarly, if one says that "what I am telling is absolutely new," then also it is absurd.

Many things are announced as new, but when they are examined in depth it is found that there is nothing new. The same things can be told in many forms, but when those forms are set aside, when the outer garbs are removed, what is found underneath is the same old thing. Thus, nowadays, neither a proclamation in favor of ancientness nor of newness can be meaningful.

In any view, the religion of the future, the one which will influence people, the one which will be followed and respected by people, will be the one that is eternal. It will neither be new nor old. No one can make it new, nor can it ever become old.

Those who call a religion old have old words to express it; those who have called it new have new words. Now we do not want to cling to any words. That is why I use words of all traditions. Any words may be of use in understanding. Sometimes I talk of the old way of thinking so that perhaps some may understand through that; sometimes I talk of the new way of thinking for those who can understand in this way. And, simultaneously, I want to remind you that truth can be neither old nor new.

Truth is eternal like the sky in which trees grow, develop, flower and then die. Trees also become old; they also have a childhood and youth. But all this is happening in the sky. We have sown a seed which has sprouted. The sprout is absolutely new, but the sky in which it has sprouted is eternal. The tree has grown, become old, and is nearing death. The tree has become old, but has the sky in which it has spread itself become old? Many a tree has come and gone, but the sky has remained there forever – eternal, untouched, unaffected. Truth then is like the sky; the words are like trees. They are sown, they sprout, they acquire leaves, flowers, fruits, and then they die, they fall back down to the ground, while the sky remains where it was.

The old and the new both have laid emphasis on words, but I do not want to lay any emphasis on words. I want only to lay emphasis on the sky in which the flowers of words open, die and become lost, no trace of them remaining anywhere. Thus, in my view, truth is eternal and is beyond the new and the old. It is transcendental.

Whatsoever we say or think or create will come and go, but truth will remain where it is. Thus, those who say that the truth is old are ignorant, because truth does not become old. And those who say, "We have a new truth, an original one," are also ignorant, because truth can be neither original nor new. Like the sky, the truth just is.

I declare this third path, the path of the eternal, to be the path for the future. Why? Because this proclamation of the eternal will cut across most of the cobwebs created by many traditions. Then we will say, "Yes, those trees grew towards the sky and these trees are also growing in the sky." Trees reach to the sky endlessly, but the sky is unaffected. There is much space in the sky. Our trees can neither fill nor empty that space. We need not remain in the illusion that any single tree can ever fill the entire sky.

Thus, none of our words, thoughts or principles can fill the sky of truth. There is always enough space. Millions and millions of Mahaviras and Buddhas, if born, would make no difference. Howsoever dense the banyan tree may be, it can make no difference to the sky. The vastness of the sky cannot be measured by the size of the banyan tree. But the blades of grass that are there under the tree do not ever know the sky; they only know the banyan tree. For them the banyan tree is so huge that they can never imagine that there can be anything greater than a banyan tree.

In this difficult situation, all the traditions have stood before us, and they have drawn our minds in all directions. There are old thoughts and new, and still newer ones are born every day. All are drawing man toward them. Because of this simultaneous pull, man's condition has become helpless. He does not know what to do. Man has almost managed to stand up, but he has no courage to walk in any direction. In no matter which direction he may attempt to take a step, he remains doubtful; he does not have any trust. All those who could have created some trust in him have themselves placed him in a condition of trustlessness.

In whatever manner trust has been created in the past, now too it is being created in the same way. The Koran continues to say that it is right, the Dhammapada says that it is right. Naturally, whoever says that he is right will have to say that the other is wrong. The other also says similarly. Thus, a person listening to both would think that all are wrong. Why? Because the one who says that he is right is only one, but those calling him wrong are fifty. The impact of being called wrong will be so strong, that the voice of one who is shouting that he is right is going to be lost in the collective voice of the fifty shouting him down as wrong.

With every one of these fifty the condition is the same, because each one is telling that he is the only right one. Now, if fifty persons call someone wrong and that someone asserts that he is right, the listener will naturally take a stand against all this nonsense.

This simultaneous demand to gain a person's trust just confuses. This situation can be corrected in only one way. There should be a worldwide movement in which no one would insist or assert that this is right or that is wrong. Instead, everyone would say that it is wrong to remain standing about inactive and it is right to walk. For this, a broad outlook is necessary which has the capacity to show correctly how one can proceed further in the direction which he has chosen. This is very difficult. It is easy to be a Mohammedan or a Christian or a Jaina because the guidelines are clear in every tradition. It is easy to be familiar with only one tradition.

One young man came to me about eight days ago. He said he is a Mohammedan and that he wants to be a sannyasin. So I advised him to be a sannyasin. But he said that his people would strangle him if he did so. I told him, "You become a sannyasin, but I do not say that you cease to be a Mohammedan. While remaining a Mohammedan, you can become a sannyasin." He said, "What! Can

I go to my mosque for *namaz*" – the Islamic way of prayer – "with these saffron clothes of a sannyasin?" I said, "Yes, you will have to do namaz."

He said, "I have left off doing namaz since I have heard you. I am doing meditation instead. I have not been going to the mosque for about one year, and I am full of joy. I do not even want to go to the mosque."

I said, "As long as you do not realize that there is no difference between meditation and namaz, I say to you that you have not understood what meditation is."

Such a person will have to be sent back to the mosque for namaz. It is very dangerous to break him away from the mosque, because after tearing someone away from the mosque it will not be possible to connect him with a temple. The method of breaking him away will damage him in such a way that he cannot be connected with any temple. Therefore, neither should we encourage any rivalry between temples, nor should we erect a new temple. Wheresoever one wishes to go, he should be free to go; he should not remain standing, but should just go.

The overall perspective which I have before me is this: that I would like to help every person to move according to his capacity, his stage of evolution, his culture – according to what has already been assimilated in his blood. Then it will be much easier for him to achieve. Therefore, I have neither any religion of my own, nor any path of my own, because now one exclusive path or religion will not work for the future, and a religious sect means a path.

Nowadays, such a religion is required which doesn't insist on a particular path, which can become the crossroads for all the paths, which can say that all paths belong to it and which can ask everyone to follow the path of his liking. Such a religion would emphasize that you will reach the same place from wherever you walk, that all roads lead to one destination, that the only insistence is that you just go on moving and do not stand still.

Therefore, I do not wish to cut a new road on the mountain, nor do I wish to create any new philosophy or religion. There are enough paths, but there are no walkers. Paths are many; the travelers are very few. The paths have been more or less unused for many years. There hasn't been any traveler because the very necessity to climb the mountain is now in doubt. There is so much debate and controversy at the base of the mountain, that the result has been only to exhaust and frighten the individual and cause him to remain standing immobile. With so much mental confusion, no one can walk.

Here, one thing must be noted. I am not eclectic. I am selective of what pleases me. My thinking is not like Gandhi's that I may select four stanzas from the Koran and four from the Gita and say that everywhere the same thing is being propounded. In both these scriptures what is told is different, not the same. I do say that by all paths one can reach the same destination, but all paths are different, not the same.

If someone attempts to show that the Koran and the Gita are telling the same thing, it is only a trick. It is very interesting to note that Gandhi would read the Gita and would read the Koran, but he would select from the Koran only such topics that did not contradict the Gita and avoid the rest. Then what will happen to those topics which are left over? Whatsoever seemed to go against anyone's beliefs would be left out by Gandhi. He would never accept the Koran as a whole, though he accepted the Gita as a whole. That is why I say that he is eclectic. If something tallying with the Gita is found in the Koran, it is accepted. For this there is no difficulty; anyone would be ready to accept.

I say that I am fully agreeable to the extent that the Koran is the Arabic translation of the Gita; nothing more than that. That much even the believer in the Koran may agree to. But it would be an interesting experiment to ask a believer in the Koran to select some verses from the Gita which may tally with the Koran. You will be surprised to find that such a person would select things which Gandhi would have never selected. He would select very different kinds of things.

This I call eclecticism. It is a selection, not an acceptance of the whole. It is like saying that selection is always one's privilege, "and if you also agree with the selection, then you are also right. Otherwise, only we are right in the end. As far as you agree with us, thus far we say that you are right, and that much tolerance we are showing."

This is not doing much. This is a matter where total acceptance is called for. It is not a matter of tolerance at all. It is not that a Hindu tolerates a Mohammedan or a Christian tolerates a Jaina. Tolerance is itself a helplessness and breeds violence at a certain stage.

I do not say that the Koran and the Gita are saying the same thing. The Koran is telling something totally different. It has its own individual tune; that is its significance. If the Koran is also saying the same thing that the Gita says, then the Koran is of no value. And the Bible is telling something still different which neither the Koran nor the Gita says. Each one has its own tune. Mahavira is not telling the same thing that Buddha tells; they talk very much differently.

But through all these different systems, the place where one reaches in the end is the same. That is why my emphasis is more on the oneness of the ultimate, not on the oneness of paths. My emphasis is on the fact that in the end all these paths reach to a place where there are no distinctions or differences.

But each path is very different, and no one should make the mistake of thinking that these paths are the same; otherwise he will not be able to walk on any of them. All the boats may reach the opposite bank, but no one should make the mistake of trying to ride two boats at a time. Otherwise the boats will reach, but never the rider of two boats. He will fall overboard and drown somewhere.

All boats are boats. So if one just wants to talk about boats from the shore, there is no harm. But a pilgrim will have to choose a boat before he can step into it. I accept all religions as different boats, but one has to be chosen.

It is very difficult to choose one because they are all contradicting each other. On one hand, there is Mahavira who would not be willing even to kill an ant; he would place his feet on the ground with the utmost care. On the other hand, there is Mohammed who is standing with a sword in hand. So anyone who tells you that Mahavira and Mohammed are saying the same thing is telling a wrong thing. These two can never talk the same language. They talk very much differently.

If an attempt is made to show them as one, then there will be grave injustice to one or the other. Either the sword of Mohammed will have to be hidden or Mahavira will have to forget about putting his feet on the ground cautiously to save the ant. So if a believer in Mohammed had to select, he would cut out all those statements of Mahavira's that go against the sword, and if a believer in Mahavira had to select, then he would take away the sword from Mohammed or would only select things that would be in consonance with non-violence.

But this is injustice. I am, therefore, not a synthesizer like Gandhi. I do not call for any synthesizing of religions. I am saying that all religions, with their own distinct individualities, are acceptable to me. I do not choose between them. I also say that because each religion is individually unique, one has a possibility of reaching.

All religions have forged their own roads, and the differences between them are only differences between the paths. It is as if along my path there are rows of trees and along your paths there are stones and stones. From the direction where you are climbing the mountain there are stones and stones, and from the direction where I am climbing there are trees and trees. One path is more difficult and exhausting to climb, with a steep gradient, while another goes up slowly, making many wide circles around the mountain. The latter path is very long, but it does not exhaust the climber.

Certainly, each climber would describe his own path differently, and the accounts of the difficulties faced on each path will be different as well as the methods to solve the difficulties. Thus, if we look at discussions about the paths, we will hardly find any similarities. And similarities which are occasionally seen are not of the paths. They are found in the statements of those who have reached the top; they are not of the paths at all.

Although the statements of those who have reached may be similar, there will be differences in language. The statements may be in Arabic, Pali, Prakrit or Sanskrit. Statements will be similar when they speak about the goal, but those statements made before reaching the goal will have very real differences. There is no need to forget about these differences.

So I do not want to cut a new path, nor do I want to proclaim that only old paths are right as against the other paths. I want to say that all paths are right, however different they may be.

Our minds are such that we think all right paths must be similar. We believe that only if two things are similar can they be right. It is not inevitable that things must be similar in order to be right. The actual truth is that if two things are similar, one is bound to be just an imitation; both cannot be original. Either one may be an imitation or both may be imitations, but at least one is bound to be an imitation. Two original things are bound to be dissimilar.

It is not surprising that there are differences between the paths of Mahavira and Mohammed. It would have been a miracle if there were no differences. It is unnatural to be similar. Mahavira's circumstances were all very much different from those of Mohammed. The people with whom Mohammed had to work were very much different from those with whom Mahavira had to work. The conditioning of the people with whom Mohammed had to work was quite different from that of the people with whom Mahavira had to work. They were so much different that it is not possible for Mahavira and Mohammed to have the same path. Even today their conditions continue to be different. One has to proceed keeping these different conditions in mind.

So neither am I anxious to cut a new path, nor am I anxious to proclaim any particular old path right as against other old paths. All paths are right – those that have been carved, those that are being carved today and those that may be carved tomorrow.

But man should only be concerned with walking and should not stand in indecision. A person who remains standing immobile on the best path will also not reach, but a person who keeps walking even on the wrong path will reach – if not today, tomorrow. The main thing is to go on walking.

If someone continues to walk, then it is not difficult to change over to the right path. But if one remains standing, then it is not possible to find out whether he is standing on the right path or not. Only by walking can one find out whether he is on the right or wrong path. If you merely believe in a certain principle while remaining indifferent, you will never know whether the principle is right or wrong. But if you put the principle to test and you experiment with it, you will immediately know whether it is right or wrong. A concept can be tested only by taking action on it, not otherwise. So I would like that you just keep on walking. I am prepared to help everyone on his own path.

Naturally, for Mahavira this was not easy to do. It is easier today, and it will go on becoming still easier because now it is almost impossible to find a person who has not been born into two, four or six religions in his last two, four or six births. Just as the world has come closer together due to faster communications during these last seven hundred years, so also it has become more possible for souls to change their religion and caste in the world. This is natural.

For example, two thousand years ago, if a *brahmin* died, the chances were ninety-nine in a hundred that he would not be reborn into a *sudra* family. Since the mind accumulates all the impressions of a life and stores them, the entry and exodus of souls was strictly conditioned by the caste system. The sudra was considered to be untouchable. Members of other castes would not even allow his shadow to fall upon them, and if such a shadow fell, immediately a bath was taken.

So the brahmin and the sudra were separated very widely – by an endless valley. After death, the brahmin's soul would not be capable of thinking to take birth in a sudra family – because the mind and its desires, which are responsible for choosing and determining one's birth, were very much against any involvement with the sudra caste. Therefore, it was not possible to change castes two thousand years ago. Up to the time of Mahavira, it was a rare phenomenon for a person to take birth in a different religion. The course of each religious tradition was so clearly defined that it flowed straight ahead like a well embanked river. Not only in one's present life, but in one's previous birth as well one would have moved within the same religious tradition.

Nowadays, in this twentieth century, this is not possible. Just as conditions have become more liberalized and farsighted in the outer world, inwardly also people have become more liberal and open-minded. It is all a matter of mind. At present it is much less embarrassing for a brahmin to sit with a Mohammedan and take his meals than it used to be, and as time passes there will be no embarrassment at all.

The person in whom this kind of embarrassment has not become less is not a modern man. His mind is five hundred years old. For the modern man there is no embarrassment at all. Nowadays, it is very absurd even to think of such embarrassment. Because of this, the doors have become wide open for souls to change religions and castes.

For the last five hundred years the doors have been opening wider and wider. Due to this, certain things can be told now. If I have walked several paths in my past births, it is now easier for me to talk about them. Thus, if some seeker from Tibet should ask me something, I would be able to guide him. But I would be able to do so only if at some time, during my chain of past births, I had come to know the value system of Tibet, if I had myself known the atmosphere that is pervading there through having lived in it; otherwise not. If I were to say anything without experience, it would only be superficial. Then it would not be deep. I would have to have passed through a particular thing myself in order to be able to tell about it in depth.

If I have not myself done any prayers in a mosque, my speaking about namaz would not be of much help. But if I have once passed through namaz myself, then I could know that one might be able to reach the same destination by namaz that one could reach by Hindu prayers. I am not then becoming eclectic. I do not say that there is no difference between namaz and *prarthana,* Hindu prayers, because I believe that Hindus and Moslems must become one. My reasons for saying so are different: I know that though the methods may differ, the goal is the same.

Thus, the situation is now changing. In the coming hundred years, there will be greater interchange among souls. Just as the outer bonds will break, so will the inner ones – in the same proportion.

You may be surprised to know that those who had imposed strict conditions on outer means and methods had actually done so only to perpetuate inner transformation. For such reasons, the caste system of this country could not be scientifically explained or understood. Nowadays we feel how much injustice must have been perpetrated by those ancient brahmins who on the one side were writing the Upanishads and on the other were planning to behave unjustly with sudras, the lowest caste. These things appear contradictory. Either the Upanishads were wrong or they could not have been written by the same brahmins who had framed the rules of conduct for the way of life for sudras. If the same brahmins have done it, there must be some mistake somewhere.

But the fact is that this arrangement has been devised by the same brahmins. You cannot imagine that the same Manu who gave the *Manu-Smriti,* the Hindu social law including the concept of the caste system, could dwell so loftily on the possibility of a human being becoming the divine. Nietzsche has said that no man more intelligent than Manu was ever born on the earth. But if we study Manu's statements on sudras and other castes, he has created tremendous insurmountable barriers between the castes such as no one else has ever done. We are not able to rock the edifice which this man built single-handed five thousand years ago. That order of society continues to remain dominant even today.

Today, all the laws, all authorities, the entire intelligentsia and the entire politics in India are ranged against this man Manu who died five thousand years ago. It is proving very difficult to remove the system which he has given. From Raja Ram Mohan Roy down to Gandhi, the wisest people in India for the last hundred and fifty years have been fighting against Manu. This man was of a great stature. Gandhi and Raja Ram Mohan Roy appear juvenile and childish before him. All conditions since Manu have changed, but yet it has been difficult to remove him. The reasons for this are inner, and they run very deep.

The basic concept was this, that if someone was doing namaz in this life, then Manu thought that that person should take birth again only in a Mohammedan family which does namaz. Otherwise, if his tradition were changed in every birth, then the work which can be completed in three births of being born in the same tradition would take thirty births. If the tradition is changed in every birth, the old links become lost. Every time a person changes the road, he has to start from ABC. He cannot be connected with his old tradition. If one was born in a Mohammedan family in the past birth and if in this birth he is born in a Hindu family, he will have to start from ABC all over again. The work done in the previous birth will be of no use.

It will be like a boy studying in the first grade who leaves a school after six months and joins another where again he starts from the beginning, and then he changes to a third school where he once more starts all over again. When will his education be complete? He will remain only in the first grade.

So Manu's concept that a person should be born again and again in the same tradition in order to enable him to start from where he had left off in the previous birth was very valuable. This could happen only if the system is made very tight and rigid, with no loopholes, no exceptions. If only this much were permitted – that it would not matter whether a brahmin married into a sudra family – then Manu was intelligent enough to see that if one can marry into a sudra family, then where is the difficulty in taking birth into a sudra family? If a brahmin, by marrying a sudra wife, can give her a child, then why can he not take a birth through a sudra mother? There is no logical objection in that case.

Therefore, if one is to be prevented from taking such a birth, he will also have to be prevented from giving such a birth. So great restrictions were placed on marriage. If the restrictions were relaxed even by an inch, the entire system that had been built would be badly disturbed.

But it has already become so. Now it will be very difficult to put it in order again – not only difficult, it will be impossible. The entire situation is such that it is not possible. Now we will have to find better methods, more subtle than those devised by Manu. Manu was very intelligent, but his system was very crude – and a crude system will prove unjust for men. The social restrictions were very much outer, though their purpose was to regulate the inner. Now this will not work. It is bound to prove difficult tomorrow if not today. It will become like a straightjacket for a society.

Now we will have to make experiments on finer planes. It means that we will have to make namaz and prarthana of such a fluid character that if one had left off from namaz in the past birth he can start prarthana in this birth just from where he had left off with namaz. Namaz and prarthana should be interchangeable. One's ears should not be so much conditioned by temple bells that the sound of *ajan,* the morning call in mosques, heard one morning seems foreign to him. Some inner harmony will have to be devised between the Hindu temple bells and the sound of ajan.

This is not difficult. For the future, there will be a necessity for a new religiousness, not a new religion. The entire concept of Manu has collapsed; the traditions of Buddha and Mahavira are lost. If one wants to experiment with the same old foundations, he will fail. Gurdjieff tried his level best to do that; Krishnamurti is laboring for this the last forty years, but nothing is happening.

All circumstances have changed. In these changed circumstances, an absolutely newly conceived concept is needed. This new concept has not been experimented upon so far. It is a concept of a new religiousness in which all religions, as they are, are right. Our eyes are to be fixed on the goal, and the insistence should be to keep on walking. One can walk on any path, but the proximity of all paths will be such that one can cross over to another path easily. The distance between the paths will not be so great that one will have to first come to the entrance of a new path if he wants to change paths. Things should be so that if he leaves one path he can cross over to the other through linking paths that join one path to another.

The goal is always connected with all of the paths, but linking paths were never there. There is no difficulty in reaching the goal through any one path, but now the times are such that one will not be able to walk on only one path. Life is becoming more and more disrupted every day, inwardly as well as outwardly.

A man born and raised in a Hindu family may have to pass his whole remaining life in Europe. Another born in America may pass his life in an Indian forest. A person brought up in London may pass the rest of his life in Vietnam. This will happen repeatedly now. The atmosphere will change daily both materially and psychologically. These changes will be so fast that we will have to construct paths that link together the highways.

The Koran and the Gita are not one, but a link can be made joining the two. So I would like to spread a network of sannyasins who are such that would form the links. These sannyasins will do namaz in a mosque, say prayers in a church and do *kirtan* in a temple also. They will walk on the path of Mahavira, meditate as Buddha did, and even experiment with the Sikh tradition, thus making connecting links – a living chain of human links. All will be struck by the one religious feeling – that all religions, though separate, are one. Not that all religions are one and inseparable, but that though they are separate, they are one in their inner harmonious march toward the goal. They are one in the sense that they lead you toward one superconsciousness.

Thus, my work is that of a third type. Such a method was never followed before. Small attempts may have been made in this direction, but they have all failed. Ramakrishna tried to do that in a small way, but that experiment is also not very old. Nearly two hundred years ago, he took his first steps in this direction. But the efforts of Ramakrishna also failed. Vivekananda again gave the effort a completely Hindu color.

Nanak also tried something in this direction about five

hundred years ago, but that also did not succeed. Nanak collected in the *Guru Grantha* the teachings of all Hindu and Mohammedan saints. Nanak used to sing, and Mardana played the *tambura*. He said that if a Hindu was singing, at least a Mohammedan should play the tambura so that sometimes the song and the instrument may become one.

Nanak went to Mecca and also prayed in the mosque, but all his efforts at integrating the two religions failed. Pantha, a new religious sect of the Sikhs, was created by collecting together all that he said in the *Guru Grantha*. Some Sufi saints tried to bring the two religions closer, but all their efforts remained confined to preliminaries and did not grow.

There were reasons for this: the era and the people had not been fully developed until that time. But now the time has come, and large-scale efforts can be made.

So my direction is the third. Neither do I want to resuscitate the old, nor do I want to create anything new. But my emphasis and insistence is only on walking – in practicing whatever there is in the old and the new.

It is your freedom to choose how you walk.

Is it possible to experience the eternal, the immortality about which You have been talking, in the conditions and circumstances of today?

THE experience of the eternal has been there for all. There is no difficulty in having the experience. The difficulty is in giving expression to the experience. Buddha had the experience of the eternal, but Mahavira was expressing it in the old language and Buddha in a new language. I want to express it in the language of the eternal itself.

You mean to ask whether I had that experience seven hundred years ago. Yes, I nearabout had the experience then, but I am giving expression to it today. When one attempts today to express whatsoever was known seven hundred years ago, there will be no difference in the knowing, but there will be a great difference in expressing it. Seven hundred years ago it could not have been told in this way; there was no reason for it.

The situation is like the appearance of a rainbow during the monsoon. This is a very interesting happening. You can see the rainbow from where you are standing. The rainbow depends on three things: drops of water from the monsoon must be present in the atmosphere and water vapor must also be there. Then also, the rays of the sun must pass through them from a particular angle, and you must be at a particular spot in order to see the rainbow. If you move away from that place, the rainbow will be lost. In the making of a rainbow, not only do the sun's rays and the drops of water meet, but your standing in a particular place is also essential. Not only do the sun's rays and the water make a rainbow, but your eyes from a particular spot contribute just as much. You are one of the three constituent elements of the rainbow. If any one of these is removed, then the rainbow will be lost.

Thus, whenever truth is revealed, three things happen. First, the experience of the truth is there. If the experience is not there, its expression is not there, its expression is not possible. Wherever you stand and whatever the drops of rain do, if the sun does not rise, there can be no rainbow. Therefore, like the existence of the sun, the existence of the experience of truth is essential. And secondly, whenever there is an experience of truth the presence of the listener must also be there. But if the person expressing is not standing at the correct angle, then nothing can be expressed.

This is what happened to Meher Baba. While expressing, Meher Baba was not able to stand at the correct angle so that a rainbow could be created between his experience and the listener. Thus, many saints remain silent. There is a reason for remaining silent, and that is that they are not able to stand at a place where they can make a proper angle for the projection of their expression. This is also necessary. Otherwise, if the speaker is not standing at the right place, the experience of truth will remain on one side and the listener will remain on the other side. But if the speaker is in the right place and capable of speaking, but the listener, who is also a necessary element, is absent, then also no expression will take place.

Seven hundred years ago, whomsoever I would speak with would also be a part of my speaking. So when I speak to you, I cannot speak the same thing that I did with that listener who existed seven hundred years ago. And if you are not sitting before me but someone else is, then too I cannot speak the same thing – because you are a basic part of what I am speaking and as much responsible for it as I am. Without you, the same thing could not be spoken. Thus, when all the three elements become attuned to the same wavelength, expression is possible.

If there is a small omission, everything is lost, the rainbow is dissolved. Then the sun does not do anything and the droplets of water in the atmosphere do not do anything. If even one of the constituent elements of the rainbow moves away, the rainbow vanishes immediately.

The expression of truth is like the existence of a rainbow. Every moment it is on the point of being lost. Even a slight shift of one thing or the other will result in its disappearance. If the listener shifts, the rainbow is lost. If the speaker shifts, the speaking will be useless.

Thus, seven days ago I would not have been able to speak the same thing that I am speaking today, nor will I be able to repeat what I am telling you today in seven days because everything will have changed by then.

The sun will remain the same; it will go on giving light. But with the exception of the sun, the truth, the other two necessary constituents, the speaker and the listener, are always capable of changing.

Therefore, the experience is that of seven hundred years ago, but the expression is of today. Even to call it of today is not proper. One should say of this moment. Even tomorrow, it will not be the same. The expression will go on changing every moment.

*Would it be possible for You to describe
what happens to the soul after death,
where it moves about, what it does
and in what condition it is during the interval
between the giving up of one body
and the taking of another?
In this connection, You had previously discussed the
freedom of the soul to take birth whenever it so desired.
Please enlighten us as to whether the soul also
has a freedom to choose whether to give up
or not give up the body.*

IT will be easier if we understand two or three things about the interval between the giving up of one body and the taking of another. First, the fact is that the experiences of that interval are like dreams. Whenever one experiences something, at that moment the experience is that of a real happening. But when one recalls it in memory, it becomes like a dream; it is dreamlike because there is no use of the senses. Your feeling and your conviction that a happening is real come through your senses and your body.

If I feel that I am seeing you, but then I try to touch you and find you cannot be touched, then I say that you are a mirage: you are not here. If I try to touch this table and if my hand passes through it without touching anything, then I would say this table is unreal, or that I am in some illusion, or that it is some hallucination. The test of reality is in the certificate of our senses.

But after the giving up of one body and before the taking of another we do not have senses. The body itself is not there, so whatever you might experience in that state is like a dream, as if you are seeing a dream. When we see dreams, we do not doubt their reality. This is very interesting. After some time we come to doubt its reality, but we never doubt it while in the dream. The dream seems real. That which is real sometimes causes us to doubt whether what is seen is real or not, but in a dream such a doubt is never created. Why? Because a dream will not tolerate the slightest doubt; otherwise it will immediately break.

A dream is such a delicate thing that a little doubt is enough to kill it. Just the feeling that it is only a dream is enough to break it, and then you will be awake. For a dream to continue, it is necessary not to have even an iota of doubt. By a slight doubt, even the deepest dream will be broken. Thus, we feel all that is seen in a dream to be a real happening. A dream appears more real than reality itself. The real can never seem so real, because it has a place for doubt. At the time of dreaming, the dream seems the most real.

In a dream, even if it is clear that something is impossible it does not appear as such. For example, in a dream some man is passing by. Suddenly he becomes a dog. You do not even think, "How can this happen?" It has happened and it is possible. There is no doubt. After waking up, you may think, "What is this nonsense?" but not until you are out of the dream. Everything is reasonable in a dream; there are no contradictions.

Someone is your friend and suddenly he aims his gun toward you. In your mind it does not occur to you to think, "How can a friend do this?" In a dream, all that is impossible becomes possible. After waking up, at the most you can remember dreams that took place only the last hour. Usually a dream becomes lost within five to seven minutes, but those who are very imaginative may, at the most, remember for not more than an hour. Otherwise, we will have so many dream memories that we will not be able to live. Within an hour the mind becomes free of dream smoke.

Just similar to this condition is the interval between two bodies. Whatever happens during that period seems absolutely real – so real that we can never know such a reality with our eyes and senses. That is why there is no end to the happiness of gods. The heavenly damsels they encounter are so real to them – real such as no woman seen through our senses can ever be. That is also why there is no end to the miseries of spirits. Their miseries befall them so realistically, such as they never do in real life.

So what we call heaven and hell are just deep dream lives. The intensity of the fire burning in hell can never be found in real life, though it is a very inconsistent fire. In scriptures, there are descriptions of the fires of hell, into which you are thrown without being burned. But one is never aware of this inconsistency — that if you were thrown into an intense fire you would not be able to withstand the heat; yet you are not in any way being burned. This inconsistency, that "I am being burned in the fire," that the fire is terrible, that the burning is unbearable and yet "I am not burned at all," is realized only after one is out of this dreamlike experience.

In the interval between two births, there are two types of souls. One type is of evil souls. For them it is difficult to find a womb for another birth. I call such souls *pretas,* evil spirits. The other type consists of good souls. Them I call *devas* – gods. For such souls also it is difficult to find suitable wombs for taking another birth.

Between these two are the majority of souls in which there is no fundamental difference, but only a difference of character, personality and mental make-up. They are of the same type; only their experiences will be different.

The evil souls return back to earth with such painful experiences that the remembering of them in itself is hell. Those who have been able to recollect such memories have described the conditions in hell. It is just a dreamland; it does not exist anywhere, but one who remembers having returned from there says that a fire such as he has seen there can find no comparison in this world, that the violence and the hatred which we find here are nothing compared to what he has seen there. The experience of heaven is also the same. The difference is only one of pleasant and painful dreams. This interval is a full dream period.

This is very philosophical but true, that it is only like a dream. We can understand what dreams are because we see them daily. You see a dream only when your senses are exhausted. In a deeper sense, it means that when your relationship with the senses breaks you sink into dream life. Dreams are also either of hell or heaven or mixed. Some people only see dreams of hell, some only of heaven.

You may think that you have seen a dream for eight hours of the night. But if this period is lengthened to eight years you will also not know, because there is no awareness of time. The hour that is passing is not clearly measured in memory. But this length of time can be measured by changes that took place in the interval between the memories of the past body and the memories of the present one.

But this is only a conjecture. During that interval, there is no clear awareness of the duration of time. Because of this, Christianity has said that there is hell forever. This is said on the basis of the memory of those who have seen a very long dream. It was such a long dream that when they returned they had no memory of any relationship between this body and the previous one. That is why they said that hell is eternal and it is very difficult to get out of it. Good souls see happy dreams and evil souls see unhappy dreams. Only because of their dreams are they feeling unhappy and miserable.

In Tibet, when a person is on his deathbed, certain matters are told to him. This is done in order to create a dream sequence. When a man dies, he is told that now he should start visualizing that which is being suggested. Thus, a new atmosphere, a new conditioning, is being created.

It is interesting, but scientific. A dream can be created from the outside. If you are sleeping at night and if a wet cloth is applied to your feet, you will have a particular type of dream. If heat is applied with a heater, another type of dream is created. If cold is applied to your feet, you may dream that is is raining or that you are walking on ice. If heat is applied to your feet, you may dream that you are walking in a desert, that there is a scorching sun and you are full of perspiration.

Thus, dreams can be created from outside. Many dreams are created as a result of outer conditions. If your hand is heavy upon your chest, you may feel that someone is riding on your chest, although it is only your own hand.

At the time of death – while giving up this body for the long period of dream life that is going to come, after which the soul may or may not take a new body – a method has been devised in Tibet for creating a dream sequence. They call this *bardo*. It is a process in which Tibetans fully prepare a person for the experience of death and life after death. Any good impulses that have been there in one's life will be aroused while the person is still living. Also, such efforts are made throughout life as well.

I told you earlier that after awaking from sleep your dream is remembered for about one hour. Similarly, after taking a new birth, for about six months, up to the age of six months, almost everything is remembered. Afterwards it slowly becomes lost. Those who are very imaginative or very sensitive may remember a little longer, but those who have made efforts and who have experimented with being aware during the previous life can remember for a long time.

Just as in the morning for one hour a dreamlike smoke revolves around you, similarly, for about one hour before falling asleep at night, the shadow of a dream begins to overcome you.

In the same way, the shadow of death also begins to fall upon you during the six months prior to your death. Your death is predictable during those six months. When the shadow of death begins to surround you during those last six months, the preparations for death are begun.

That one hour before sleep, when the dream shadow begins falling upon you, is a very suggestible one. No other time is as suggestible, because at that time you have a doubt that you are still awake and the shadow of sleep is overtaking you. That is why all the religions of the world have decreed one hour before sleeping at night and one hour after awaking in the morning as the best times for prayers. It is known as *sandhyakal* – the twilight time and the time of dawn.

Sandhyakal does not mean the time when the sun is setting or rising. It means the time when from wakefulness you are passing into sleep and from sleep you are passing into wakefulness. This in-between period is sandhyakal. The sun has nothing to do with it, but it has become associated with the sun from those days when the setting of the sun signified the time to sleep and the rising of the sun the time to wake up. But now this association must be broken because no one sleeps at sunset, nor does anyone rise with the sun. Actually speaking, sandhyakal means an hour before sleeping and an hour after waking. It means a period of time in between the two conditions of waking and sleeping.

Kabir has called his language *sandhya-bhasha* – the twilight-and-dawn language. He has said that neither do we speak as if we are asleep, nor do we speak as if we are awake. We are just in the middle. We are in such difficulty that neither are we speaking from within ourselves nor from outside ourselves. We are standing in the middle, on the borderland, from where we are able to see what the eyes can see and also what the eyes cannot see. We are just on the threshold. So that which we are speaking includes that which cannot be said as well as all which can be spoken. That is why ours is a twilight-and-dawn language. Its meanings must be drawn very carefully.

That one-hour period in the morning and one-hour period in the night before sleeping is very valuable. Similarly, the six-month period after birth and the six-month period before death are equally valuable. But those who do not know the use of the one-hour twilight-and-dawn periods do not understand the importance and value of these six-month periods.

When there were civilizations which were very knowledgeable about these things, then the first six months after birth were known to be very important. Everything that is important can be given to the child in the first six months of life. In the first six months the child is suggestible and in its dawn period. After that, it is not possible and it becomes very difficult.

But we cannot make him understand by speaking. And because we do not know any other method but speaking, there are difficulties. Similarly, the six months before death are also valuable. In the first six months we cannot make a child understand our speech, and we do not know when the last six months before death have come. Thus, we lose both the opportunities.

But a person who utilizes properly the one hour before sleep and the one hour after waking will positively know when that six-month period before death begins. One who prays and meditates for one hour before sleep will clearly be able to feel when this twilight time before death has come. This is such a fine and subtle experience that it is neither like sleeping nor like waking. This experience is so fine and different that once it is properly understood one can become aware of the beginning of that six-month period before death – because then the feeling of twilight will persist throughout the day. The experience and the feeling which was previously coming for only one hour before sleep will remain continuous and steady during these last six months.

That is why the last six months before death should be fully utilized for sadhana. The same six months are utilized by the Tibetans for bardo – for a type of dream training which is given to plan what you will do after death. This training cannot be given just at the moment of death. It requires preparation, and only a person who is ready during these last six months can be trained during the first six months after birth in the next life; otherwise it is not possible. Those principles which are taught during these last six months lay the foundation for the training which can be given in the first six months of the new birth.

All these things have their own scientific thinking, their principles and their secrets. And everything can be tested as well. A person who has passed through this training would also remember what happened in the interval between two births, but this memory is the memory of a dream; it is not real.

Heaven and hell are also memories of a dream period. Descriptions can be given. It is only on such descriptions that concepts of heaven and hell have been evolved by all religions. The descriptions are different not because the places are different, but because the mental states of the individuals recalling the experiences are different. Therefore, when Christianity describes heaven, it will be different from what Hinduism will describe, because descriptions depend on different states of consciousness. Thus, the Jainas will describe it still differently and Buddhists also.

Actually, every person will bring back a different story. It is more or less like when we all sleep in the same room and then get up and describe our dreams. We have slept in the same room; we are at the same place, but our dreams will be different. Everything depends upon the person.

All experiences of heaven and hell are individual, but broad similarities can be found – that there will be happiness in heaven and misery in hell, that such and such will be the form and shape of miseries and such and such will be the form and shape of happiness. All the descriptions that have been given thus far are, in a way, faithful narrations of different states of consciousness.

It has been asked, "If a person can choose his birth, can he also choose his death?" Here also two or three things will have to be remembered. The freedom to choose one's birth means that if one so desires he can take birth. This is the first freedom of a person who has reached supreme knowledge. If he desires, he can take birth. But no sooner is there a desire when the slavery begins with that very desiring.

I am standing outside a building. I have the freedom to enter the building if I want. But as soon as I enter the building, the limitations of the building immediately begin to influence my movements. Therefore, the freedom to choose death is not as great as the freedom to choose one's birth.

For an ordinary person, there is no freedom to choose death because he has not even chosen his birth. But the freedom of the one who is realized to choose his birth is total, and it is a very great one in the sense that he can also refuse to take birth if he so desires. But once the choice to take birth is made, a number of bondages begin coming into play – because he chooses limitations. He gives up the unlimited space and enters the narrow passage. The narrow passage imposes its own limitations.

Now he chooses a womb. Ordinarily, one doesn't choose his womb. But when a realized person chooses, he has to make a choice from hundreds of thousands of such wombs that are available. He chooses out of them; from among those he chooses. But no sooner does he choose than he enters the world of bondage. All wombs have their limitations. He chooses one mother and one father. In the process, he has chosen the same longevity as had the fertilized eggs of his parents. The selection has been made, and now he will have to use this body.

If you go to the market and purchase a machine with a ten-year guarantee, the limit is set. The machine is knowingly purchased, so there is no question of slavery. You do not say, "I purchased this machine, and now I am enslaved because it will only last for ten years." You have chosen in full knowledge that it will last for ten years, and so the matter ends. There is no sense of pain or sting in this.

The one who takes birth consciously knows when the body will die, so he has the awareness of a death-oriented body. In such persons there is a sort of impatience which is not to be seen in ordinary people. If we study the story of Jesus, we will feel that he is very impatient, as if something is going to happen to him in just a few moments. Those who are listening to him do not understand his difficulties because they are not very much aware of their own approaching death. But for Jesus, death is standing in front of him; he knows when it is going to happen.

Jesus asks you to complete the work today, and you say you will do it tomorrow. Then Jesus is in a difficulty because he may not be there tomorrow. Therefore, whether it is Mahavira or Buddha or Jesus, they are in a hurry. They are running at great speed because among so many dead people they are the ones who are aware of everything. Therefore, such individuals are always in a hurry. It would not make any difference if such realized ones could live to a hundred or two hundred years of age, because any length of time is short for them. We do not find time short because we do not know when it will end. We even keep on forgetting that it will end.

The freedom to choose one's birth is a very great one, but birth itself is an entry into a jail, and all the limitations of the jail will have to be accepted. But such a person accepts these things naturally because it is his choice. If he has come to a jail, he is not brought there; he has come by himself. Therefore, he stretches out his hands for chains to be put on. In these chains there is no sting, no pain. He sleeps near dark walls without any difficulty because he has come into the prison out of his own free will. He could have stayed under the open sky, but he has come to the prison out of his own free will.

When slavery is by choice it is freedom, but if freedom is without choice it is slavery. Freedom and slavery are clearly demarcated entities. If we have chosen slavery of our own will it is freedom, but if freedom is imposed upon us it is slavery. For one who has taken birth consciously, things are seen very clearly, and so he makes his decisions with ease. He knows that he will live for seventy years, so he decides clearly what he has to do within that time. He picks up only such things which he can complete; he does not spread his net too far into the future. Whatsoever he can do just tomorrow, he will do – and he will complete it; that is why he does not ever remain in anxiety.

As he goes on living, he is preparing to die also. Death is also a preparation for him. In one sense he is in a hurry – as far as others are concerned. Where he himself is concerned he is not in any hurry. For himself nothing remains to be done. He can even choose how he will die. If he has to die within the limits of seventy years, he is able to decide what momentum to give to the body – when, how and in what manner he will die.

There was one Zen nun. She had informed people that she would die after six months. She prepared for herself a pyre on which her body was to be burned. On the appointed day she climbed upon it, bowed to all those standing around her, and then some of these friends set fire to the funeral pyre. When the flames of the fire came near her, someone from the crowd asked, "Aren't you feeling very hot?"

The nun laughed and said, "What a fool you are! Even at this last opportunity you are asking such silly questions. You could have asked something useful and important. I know and you know also that if I sit within the flames I will feel hot."

But this was her choice. She was laughing while she was being burned. She had selected even the moment of her death, and she wanted to teach the disciples standing around her that it is possible to die laughing. For those who are not even able to live laughing, this message that one can even die laughing is very important.

Death also can be well planned, but what the choice will be will depend upon the one who is choosing. However, this is all within limits. If I have to remain within this room, I can decide in which corner I will sit – whether to sleep on the left side or the right side; such is my freedom. Such a person makes use even of his death and makes use of everything in his life. Sometimes such use may be apparent, sometimes not. In fact, he takes birth *only* to be useful to others. For himself there is no need. Becoming useful to others is his purpose. But it is very difficult for us to understand his experiments. Usually, we are not able to understand them. Whatsoever he is doing, we are not aware of it. It cannot be done with our knowledge.

Now, a person like Buddha will never say, "I will die tomorrow." If the time when he has to die is tomorrow, it is of no use to tell it today. Then that which could be done today will also not get done. Then people will begin to cry and weep even from today. Then even these next four hours cannot be usefully spent. So such a person will remain silent for some time, but later on he may proclaim his death aloud. However, he will decide according to the prevailing situation.

From womb to tomb, the birth after self-realization is one of training. But this training is not for the enlightened one's sake. It is a discipline, but not for his own sake. The strategy will have to be changed constantly because all strategies become old and burdensome and become difficult for people to understand.

For example, Gurdjieff: he would first make you pay a hundred dollars before he would answer your question, while Mahavira would not even touch any money. And Gurdjieff would reply only in one or two sentences. If another question were to be asked, he would make the questioner pay another hundred dollars. Many times people asked him what he was doing. Those who knew him were puzzled because one moment it appeared as if he was going to keep the money and the next he would distribute it to others. Why then demand a hundred dollars?

Gurdjieff said that to tell those who have valued only money in life anything about God free of charge would be of no value. Such people cannot evaluate things that are received without payment. Gurdjieff meant that for receiving anything of value, one will have to pay something in return one way or the other. One who is not ready to pay anything has no right to receive.

But people thought that Gurdjieff loved money because he would not reply without receiving a payment. As I see it, in the West where he lived, where people could only value money, only such a teacher could be effective. He knew that when you have shown a readiness to pay for every word, then you have known its value. You will only take home what you have paid for, not something that is received free.

Gurdjieff would do things the likes of which you would not approve. His disciples would be embarrassed. They would tell him that if he would refrain from such actions it would be better. But Gurdjieff would do them knowingly and intentionally. He would be sitting, and if you went to see him he would make faces as if he were a villain. He would not look like a saint at all. Having experimented for a long time on Sufi methods, he could suddenly make his eyes squint and change into cunning expressions.

His whole appearance changed with the change in the angle of his eyes. Between a saint and a villain there is not much difference in appearance except in the angles of their eyes. As soon as this is changed, a saint can look like a villain and vice versa.

Gurdjieff's eyes were very shifty and quick-changing. Even the person who was sitting beside him would not know that he had frightened the newcomer. The newcomer would be so much frightened that he might feel like running away. When Gurdjieff's friends came to know of this, they asked him why he was behaving in this way. Even before they came to know anything about that newcomer, the newcomer would be frightened off. Why?

Gurdjieff would then explain that the newcomer would have found a villain in him even if he were a saint; it would have taken him some time though. But Gurdjieff did not want him to waste his time, so he showed him what he had come to look for and indicated that he may now go away, because he would have unnecessarily wasted his three or four visits only to find the same thing.

But if a newcomer would remain unmoved in spite of such behavior, only then would Gurdjieff have tried to do some work on him. Thus, if he had really come to know truth, he would wait patiently and not come to hasty conclusions.

So it depends upon the teacher how he wants to teach. Sometimes even for his whole life, it is not possible for you to know his purpose. The teacher utilizes every moment of his life from birth to death. He doesn't even waste a single moment. His every moment is deeply meaningful, and it is part of a grand purpose and a great destiny.

4

THIS IS A TIME OF CRISIS

March 12, 1971

You have told us what happens to the soul during that timeless interval between two births.
But some points remain unresolved, regarding the bodiless soul: in that bodiless state, does the soul remain stationary or can it move about?
And how does it recognize other souls?
In that state, is there any possibility of a dialogue between souls?

IN this connection, two or three things may be remembered. Firstly, neither is there any stationary condition nor any movement in that state. That is why it becomes even more difficult to understand. It is easy for us to understand that if there is no movement there must be a state of rest or vice versa. In our thinking, these are the only two possibilities for everything. We think that in the absence of one the other must prevail. We are also under the impression that these two states are opposite to each other.

So firstly, we should understand that movement and non-movement are not opposites, but different aspects of the same thing. When the movement is such that we are not able to see or grasp it, we call it non-movement. Movement is, likewise, a state of non-movement which we are not able to comprehend. If something moves at a great speed, you will find that it appears stationary.

If a fan is moved at a high speed, you will not be able to see the blades. At that speed, you will not be able even to tell how many blades the fan has, because the empty space between the three blades becomes filled before we can see it. A fan can move so quickly that you cannot put anything through the spaces between the blades. Things can be moved in such a way that even if you touch them with your hand you will feel that they are not moving. That is why science says that all things that appear stationary to us are also moving, but the movement is very fast and at levels that are beyond the grasp of our senses. Therefore, movement and non-movement are not two things. They are different states of the same thing differing only in degree.

In the realm where there is no body, both these conditions will not be there because where there is no body there is neither time nor space. From what we have known thus far, it is not possible for us to conceive of a realm beyond time and space because we have not known anything that is beyond.

What then shall we call that condition? We do not even have any word to express a condition where there is no time and space. When, during a religious experience, messages of such a state were received for the first time, difficulties arose regarding how to describe it. What is the name of that state? An embarrassment similar to this is also experienced by science when it has difficulty in naming a newly discovered phenomenon; when something happens which is different from and beyond all our pertinent knowledge, this becomes very difficult.

For example, some years ago, when the electron was first discovered, the question arose whether to call it a particle or a wave. We cannot call it a particle because matter is always static; nor can we call it a wave because a wave is always moving and is weightless. The electron is both simultaneously. Then difficulty arises – because in our understanding a thing can be only one of the two, but not both. But the electron is both a particle as well as a wave. Sometimes we comprehend it as a particle, sometimes as a wave. There is no word in any language of the world to express this phenomenon.

For the scientists who observed this, it seemed inconceivable. It became a mystery. When people asked Einstein why he was describing the electron as both a particle and a wave, they felt that his thinking was becoming illogical and mysterious. Einstein, in reply, then asked them whether he should believe fact or logic. The fact is that the electron is both at the same time, but logic tells us that a thing can be only one at a time. A man is either standing or walking. Logic tells us that he can be one thing at a time; he cannot be both standing and walking simultaneously. Logic, therefore, will not agree. But the experience of the electron required that scientists should put aside logic and hold fast to facts. The electron is an example.

The experience of religious individuals tells us that during that interval between the leaving of one body and the taking of another, the bodiless soul is neither stationary nor in movement. This is beyond our understanding. That is why some religions say the bodiless soul is stationary and others say that it is in movement. But this is only due to the difficulty of explaining – because the boundaries of space and time within which movement or non-movement is observed do not exist during that interval. For both movement or non-movement, a body is necessary. Without body, there can be neither movement nor non-movement. The body is the only medium through which these conditions can be observed.

For example, this is my hand. I can either move it or keep it steady. Someone may ask, when I do not have this physical hand, whether or not my soul will be moving. The question itself is meaningless because without this hand the soul can neither move nor remain stationary. Movement and non-movement are both qualities of the body. Beyond body, the words movement and non-movement have no meaning.

This is applicable to all dualities. Take, for example, the condition of speaking and the condition of remaining silent. Without the body, it is neither possible to speak nor to remain silent. Ordinarily, we can understand that it is not possible to speak without body, but it is difficult to understand that it is not possible even to be silent without body. Through the medium which enables one to speak, one can express silence as well. Becoming silent is only a way of speaking, a state of speaking. Silence is not only a state of not speaking, but of speaking as well.

For example, a man is blind. One may feel that perhaps he is only able to see darkness. This is illusion. Even to see darkness, eyes are necessary. Without eyes, it is not possible even to see darkness. You may close your eyes and think that because you are seeing darkness it is possible, but you are making a mistake. While you close your eyes, your eyes do not cease to be there; you do not become blind. If you become blind after once having had eyes, then you will know what darkness is. But for the one who is blind since birth it is not possible to know what darkness is, because darkness is also an experience of eyes. You experience darkness with the same medium used to experience light. One who is blind since birth cannot know what darkness is.

You hear through your ears. In language, we may say that one who has no ears is not hearing. But that state of not hearing is also not known to those who are deaf. Ears are necessary even to know that you did not hear. It is just like eyes being necessary to know what darkness is. Non-movement is possible only through that sense in which there is movement. If there is no sense, there is no experience of non-movement. In the bodiless state, the soul can neither speak nor remain silent. There is no instrument for speaking or for remaining silent. All experiences are dependent on the instrument – on the body, on the senses.

But this does not mean that such a bodiless soul has reached liberation. The descriptions of a soul in liberation and one that is in the interval between life and rebirth may appear similar. What then is the difference between the liberated soul and the one that is in this interval? The difference is of potentiality, of seed existence.

During the bodiless existence, the interval between two bodies, the experiences and impressions of all previous births remain with the soul in seed form. As soon as the soul acquires a body, they will become active. For example, if we cut the feet of a person, his experiences of running will not disappear. Without feet he can neither run nor stop, because if he cannot run how can he stop? But if he acquires feet, all of his experiences and impressions will become active again and he will be able to run if he wants to.

It is like taking away a car from a person who has always been driving. Now he cannot drive a car or press an accelerator – because he has no car. Neither can he apply brakes to slow down. But his experiences of car driving remain with him. He is out of the car, but his experiences of driving remain with him in seed form. If he acquires a car after some years, he will be able to drive it as soon as he puts his foot on the accelerator.

The liberated soul becomes free of these impressions, whereas in the interval between two bodies the soul only becomes free of the senses, the instruments. In liberation, all experiences, impressions and desires are destroyed. In both conditions of the soul, there is one similarity – that there is no body. But there is one dissimilarity. In liberation there is neither body nor the chain of bodily experiences. In the interval between births, though there is no body, there is a great chain of body-related experiences existing in seed form which can become active at any time upon acquisition of a body.

So whatever experiences one may have in this interval will be such as can be had without body. As I have said, these will be experiences of meditation. But the experiences of meditation are had only by very few persons. Out of millions of people, only one has that experience of meditation. What experiences can the remaining people have? Their experiences will be of a dream life. In a dream, no sense participates.

It is possible that if a person is in a dream, and if you can keep him in the dream and cut off his limbs, his dream may not be disturbed. But the chances are that his sleep will break. If it were possible to cut off his limbs one after the other without breaking his sleep, then his dream would continue undisturbed because none of the limbs of the body are necessary for the dream. The body is not at all active in a dream; there is no use of the body in it. Without the body the dream experience will remain. In fact, all experiences will remain in dream form.

If someone were to ask you whether you are stationary or in movement during a dream, you would find it difficult to reply. When you awake from the dream, you find that all along you were lying in the same place, but you were in a dream. Upon waking, you find that there have been long, deep happenings in the dream, but, remember, there was no movement at all in it.

If you understand properly, you will find that you are not even a participant in a dream. In a deep sense, you can only be a witness. That is why one can see oneself dying in a dream; one can see one's own body lying dead. In a dream, if you see yourself walking, then the one whom you see walking is a dream phenomenon and you are but a witness.

That is why religion has put forth the idea that if a person can view this world like a dream he will have the highest religious experience. From this only, the theological concept of calling this world *maya* – an illusion or a dream – has been put forth. The deeper meaning of this is that if one can view the world as if in a dream, then one becomes a witness. In a dream, one is always a witness and no one is a participant. In no circumstances are you ever an actor. Though you may see yourself as an actor, you are always the spectator, the seer, the one who is seeing.

Therefore, all bodiless experiences will be like dreams – seed-like. Those whose experiences have created misery for them will see nightmares and dreams of hell. Those whose experiences have brought them happiness will dream of heaven and will be happy in their dreams. But these are all dreamlike experiences.

Sometimes different types of events may also happen, but these kinds of experiences will differ. Occasionally, it may so happen that souls which are neither stationary nor in movement will enter other bodies. But to say that the souls will enter is a linguistic fallacy. It would be better to say that some body may behave in such a way that it will cause a soul to enter into it. The world of such souls is not different from ours. That world exists also beside us, close by. We are all residing in the same world. Every inch of space that is here is filled with souls. The space right here which appears empty to us is also full.

There are two types of bodies which are in a state of deep receptivity. One is of those that are in great fear. Those who are in great fear cause their souls to contract within their bodies – so much so that they vacate some parts of the body completely. Some nearby souls drift into these empty parts like water entering a ditch. At such times, these souls experience things that only a soul with a body can experience.

Secondly, a soul can enter a body when it is in a deep prayerful moment. In such prayerful moments also, the soul contracts. But during fearful moments, only such souls drift in which are in great misery and agony, that see only nightmares. Those are the ones whom we call evil spirits. Because a frightened person happens to be in an ugly and dirty state, no higher soul can enter him.

A fearful person is like a ditch: only downward moving souls can enter. A prayerful person is like a peak: only upward moving souls can enter. A prayerful person becomes filled with so much inner fragrance and so much inner beauty that only the highest souls take interest in him. And such higher souls will enter only by what we call invocation, invitation or prayer.

Both these types of experiences by souls are such as could be had only with body. Thus, there is a complete science for invoking *devatas* – gods. These devatas do not descend from some heaven, nor do those whom we call evil spirits come from hell or some devil's world. They are all present right here, coexisting with us.

Actually, in the same space, there is a multidimensional existence. For example, this room where we are sitting is full of air. If someone burns some incense, some aromatic substance, the room will become filled with fragrance. If someone sings a melodious song, sound waves will also fill the room. But the smoke of the incense will not clash with the waves of the song. This room can be filled with music as well as with light, but no light wave will clash with any sound wave. Nor will the light waves have to leave to make room for the entry of sound waves.

In fact, this very space is filled in one dimension by sound waves, in another by light waves and in a third dimension by the air waves. Likewise, hundreds of things fill this room in hundreds of different dimensions. They do not in any way hinder one another, nor does any one thing have to move out of the way for something else. Therefore, all this space is multidimensional.

For example, in this place we have a table, but we cannot keep another table in the same place because tables are of the same dimension. But an existence of another dimension will not find the table to be a barrier. All these souls are very much near us; any time there can be an entry. When the souls enter, then they will have a bodily type of experience, and these experiences are such as can be had only through body.

Another factor concerns the way in which these souls that enter living bodies communicate. Communication is possible only between the soul entering and the soul existing in the body. That is why, so far on this earth, no spirit, evil or godly, has been able to communicate directly with us, right before our very eyes. But it is not true there has not been any communication. Communication takes place. Information that we have about heaven and hell is not something out of people's imaginations, but it has been communicated by such souls through mediums.

Thus, in olden times, there was a system. For example, with the Vedas of the Hindus, none of the rishis of the Vedas would ever say that he was the writer of such and such a Veda; in fact, he was not a writer at all. It is not out of humility or modesty that the rishis did not claim to be the writers. It is a fact that what they had written down was, in a sense, *heard* by them. This is a very clear experience: when some soul enters into you and speaks, the experience is so clear that you know full well you are sitting aside while someone else and not you is speaking. You too are the listener and not the speaker.

This is not easy to know from outside, but if observed with proper attention it is possible. For example, the manner and style of speech will be different, the tone will differ, the diction and the language will also differ. To the original owner of the body, everything will be crystal clear from inside. If some evil spirit has entered, then the person will perhaps be so much afraid that he will become unconscious. But if a celestial soul has entered, then he will be aware and awakened such as he never was before. Then the situation will be crystal clear to him.

So those in whom the evil spirits enter will be very clear about the fact that someone had entered into them only after such evil spirits leave the body – because they become so fearful that they faint and fall unconscious. But those in whom celestial souls enter will be able to say at the very moment that "what is being spoken is by someone else, not by me."

Just as two persons may use only one microphone, both these voices will use the same instrument. One will stop speaking while the other will start. When the senses of the body can be so used, it is possible for bodiless souls to communicate. That is how whatever is known to this world about devas and evil spirits becomes communicated. There is no other way to know about these things.

For all this, complete sciences have been evolved. Once a science is evolved, things become easier to understand. Then these things can be made use of with full understanding. When these kinds of events happened in the past, scientific principles were derived from them. For example, if accidentally and suddenly some celestial soul had entered into someone, then from the study of that happening certain principles regarding the conditions conducive for such a phenomenon would be evolved. Then it could be said that if such conditions can be created again, then again such souls will enter.

For example, Mohammedans will burn *lohban*. This is a method of inviting good spirits by creating a specific fragrant atmosphere. Hindus also burn incense, and they light a flame made from ghee. These things appear to be ritualistic formalities today, but at one time they had a deep meaning.

Hindus will chant a specific mantra which becomes an invocation. It is not necessary that there should be a meaning to the mantra. Ordinarily there is none, because mantras with meaning become distorted with the passage of time. But meaningless mantras do not become distorted. With a meaningless mantra nothing extraneous can enter with the passage of time. That is why all mantras of depth are meaningless. They have no meaning, so they remain changeless. They are only sounds. There are methods for the chanting of these sounds. If there is a specified beat, intensity and rhythm, the soul that is invoked will enter instantly. And if the soul for whom the mantra was devised is dissolved into nirvana, another soul of similar purity will enter.

All the religions of the world have certain mantras. The Jainas have *Namokar*.

I bow down to those who have destroyed all enemies.
I bow down to those who have achieved liberation.
I bow down to those who are the religious preceptors.
I bow down to those who are the priests.
I bow down to all the religious aspirants.

It has five divisions. On each division there is an invocation which becomes deeper and deeper.

Ordinarily, people chant the entire mantra, but this is not the proper way. Those who desire to contact high souls should go on repeating only the first part. The remaining four parts need not be repeated. There should be full emphasis on one part only because the souls related to that part are different from those related to other parts.

For example, the first part of this mantra, *Namo Arihantanam,* is a prostration to the *arihantas* – those who have destroyed all enemies and those who have transcended all their senses. *Ari* means an enemy and *hanta* means the destroyer. Therefore, this is a particular invocation to fully enlightened souls who can take only one birth more. This one part should be repeated with a special sound and impact. In this invocation, other Jaina souls are not included and, therefore, they cannot be contacted.

This *arihant* is a special technical word which is connected with the highest Jaina souls. With this mantra, the soul of Jesus Christ cannot be contacted; there is no such desire expressed here. With this mantra, even Buddha cannot be contacted. This is a technological term for the invocation of a particular category of Jaina souls. Like this, in all the five separate parts of Namokar, there is an invocation for five different categories of souls.

The last invocation, *Namo loye savva sahunam,* is for invoking all the religious aspirants. It is directed to all aspirants of all religions; it has nothing to do with the Jainas or any specific group other than Jainas. It is a very generalized invocation for contact with any religious aspirant without any particularization.

All religions have such mantras through which contacts have been made. These mantras became *shakti-mantras,* and they became highly significant. A mantra is like a name given to a person, such as the name Ram. When the person is called by the name, immediately he becomes alert.

So there are also mantras for ordinary spirits. There are sciences for invoking both ordinary and extraordinary souls. Sometimes it may not be possible to contact a particular soul who is invoked because he may not be there due to the lapse of time. But it will always be possible to contact souls of a similar type with a mantra.

Now take the example of Mohammed. He always said that he was only a *paigambara,* a messenger, because Mohammed never felt that whatever he was experiencing was his own. The voice which came to him from above was very clear. His experiences are described by Mohammedans as *ilham* – revelations. Mohammed felt that something entered into him and began speaking. He himself could not believe the happening. He did not think that anyone else would believe him. If he were to say that what was spoken was spoken by himself, he thought that no one else would believe him because he had never spoken that way before. He was not known to the people to speak in such a way. People did not know that he could tell such things, so he knew that no one would believe such a story.

He came back home from the place where the revelation took place in a mood of great fear, trying to avoid others and escape being seen. He did not want to reveal immediately what he knew, because then people would not trust him as he did not have a background for such things in his earlier life. Upon coming home he told his wife what had happened. He also told her that if she was able to trust him, then he would tell it to someone else – otherwise not, because that which had come to him had come from above. Someone had spoken to him; it was not his voice. But when his wife trusted him, he began telling others.

With Moses too, the same thing happened. The voice descended upon him. In order for this voice to descend, some great divine spirit must use someone as a medium. But everyone cannot be used as a medium. This capacity and purity to become a vehicle, a medium, is not a minor thing. Communication can only be possible if a capable vehicle is available. For such communication, another's body has to be used.

This type of attempt was made in recent times with Krishnamurti, but it failed. This is the story of the attempted reincarnation by Buddha under the name of Maitreya. Buddha had said that he would take one more birth, with that name. A great deal of time had elapsed – about two thousand five hundred years – but still Buddha did not take birth. Indications had been received that Maitreya was not able to find a suitable mother or womb. Therefore, a different type of attempt was made. If it was not possible to find a suitable mother or womb, some selected individual might be developed and made ready through whom Maitreya could speak whatever he wanted to.

For this purpose, the large Theosophical movement was started – to arrange for the selection of a suitable individual and prepare him in every way to deserve to be the vehicle for Maitreya. The soul which wanted to give a message through Mohammed found in Mohammed a ready-made vehicle; he did not have to prepare anyone. Even the soul that gave a message through Moses did not have to make a vehicle. They found the vehicles ready-made. Those times were simple, and people were more innocent and less filled with ego. It was easy to find a vehicle then because one could, in full humility, surrender one's body to another soul for use, as if that body did not belong to him.

But now it is impossible. Individuality has become rigid and ego-centered; no one wants to surrender. Therefore, the Theosophists selected four or five small children – because it could not be confidently predicted how each child would develop. They selected Krishnamurti as well as his brother Nityananda. Afterwards, they also selected Krishnamenon and also George Arundale.

Nityananda died a premature death as a result of the intensive preparations to make him the medium for Maitreya. Krishnamurti became so mentally disturbed by his brother's death that he himself could not become the medium.

Krishnamurti was selected at the age of nine by Annie Besant and Leadbeater. But this world is a big drama; this experiment was done by great powers. The drama was played on an international stage by powerful individuals. When the possibility of Maitreya entering into Krishnamurti became very near, certain, the soul of Devadatta who had been Buddha's cousin, and who had for his whole life opposed Buddha and attempted several times to kill him, influenced the mind of Krishnamurti's father.

Thus, a legal suit influenced by Devadatta was filed by Krishnamurti's father against Annie Besant and the other Theosophists, demanding back the possession of his son Krishnamurti who had been in their custody. This suit was fought up to the Privy Council. This fact has not been told before. I am telling it for the first time: Annie Besant fought the legal battle tooth and nail. But in the law courts, it was not possible for her to win because it was the father's right to claim possession of his minor child. Even if the child were to refuse to go to the father it was not possible for him to win because he was a minor. Therefore, it was necessary for them to run away from India taking Krishnamurti with them. In India the suit was going on, and Annie Besant ran away out of India with Krishnamurti. The suit went on up to the Supreme Court; there

Annie Besant was defeated. It was a legal battle and Devadatta was more powerful.

Ordinarily, the law becomes more cooperative in the hands of the criminal because a good man is not preoccupied with matters of law. The criminal first makes all the necessary arrangements for his legal battle.

Afterwards, Annie Besant appealed the case to the Privy Council in London, and there the decision was reversed, against all legal provisions, to let the child remain with Annie Besant. There had never been any such precedent before, nor was the judgment just and proper. But there was no further appeal beyond the Privy Council. This judgment was made possible by the influence of the soul of Maitreya who did not interfere in the lower courts or the appellate courts. He reserved his powers of influence for the last court of appeal.

Thus, on the lower plane, it was an enacted drama witnessed by big headlines in newspapers and legal battles fought in law courts. But on the higher plane, a great battle was fought between two powerful souls. Afterwards, such great pains were taken in Krishnamurti's preparation that had, perhaps, never been taken before with any other individual. Individuals may have taken greater pains in preparing themselves for certain achievements, but so many people had never staked so much on one person.

But in spite of all this great effort, when the time came all hopes fell through. Theosophists had gathered some six thousand people in Holland from all over the world, and it was scheduled to be announced that Krishnamurti had on that day given up his own personality and accepted that of Maitreya. All the preparations were made. The long awaited moment came when he was to climb up to the rostrum to announce that he was no more Krishnamurti, so that the soul of Maitreya might enter and begin to speak. Six thousand delegates from all over the world had gathered together from far and wide, in great expectation, to listen to the voice of Maitreya. A great unprecedented event was to take place.

But nothing happened. At that crucial moment, Krishnamurti

refused to relinquish his individuality. Devadatta had made his final attempt, and what could not be done in the Privy Council was made possible in that last court of the delegates. He made Krishnamurti announce that he was not a teacher – not a world teacher, that he had nothing to do with anyone else's soul, that he was what he was, and that he did not want to tell anything more. A great experiment failed. But in one sense, it was the first experiment of its type, and there was a greater possibility of failure.

So it is not possible for souls to communicate unless they can enter into someone's body. That is why a birth as a human being is indispensable. For example, someone dies now, and if he remains in a bodiless state for a hundred years there is no development of any type whatsoever during the hundred years. He will begin in the new birth from where he was when he died in the previous life – right from there – no matter how long the intervening period may be. This intervening period is not a time of development. It is like waking up in the same bed where you had slept the previous night.

That is why many religions went against sleep, because during sleep there is no progress. These religions began to reduce the sleeping time because of lack of development during sleep. You get up in the same bed you had slept in, unchanged. Exactly the same way, when you take birth again you pick up from where you had left off when you died. There is no change in your condition. It is like my stopping the watch now, but when I start it again it will start exactly from where it had stopped.

In the interval between births, all development is blocked. That is why no devatas can reach salvation while in heaven – because there is no action there; one cannot do anything there. There one can only dream endlessly. For doing something, one has to take a human birth on earth.

Also, in regard to souls recognizing each other, two spirits desiring to meet each other can do so only by entering into two different bodies. There is no way of direct recognition. It is like twenty persons sleeping in this room. They will remain the whole night in the same room, but in sleep there is no way for them to know one another. They can know one another only after waking.

When we wake up, our recognition continues – but in sleep it is not possible; there we have no relationship whatsoever. It is possible that one person may wake up and see all the rest that are sleeping. This means that if one soul enters into someone's body that soul can see the other souls. But the other souls cannot see that one soul.

If one soul enters into somebody's body, it can know something about the other souls that are bodiless. But those bodiless souls cannot know anything. Actually, the fact of knowing and recognizing is possible only through a brain residing in a body, and upon death the body dies together with its brain.

But there are some other possibilities. If some persons have experimented while living, and have established relationships through telepathy or clairvoyance, which are methods of knowing without use of the brain and which have nothing to do with the brain, then such persons may succeed in establishing relationships with evil spirits as well as celestial souls. But there are very few persons of that capacity. However, information about the conditions prevailing in the spiritual world has been given to us only by such souls.

The situation is like this: twenty people drink liquor and all become unconscious. But among them one person who had a long habit of drinking could remain fully conscious, and so he could tell about the experiences of being drunk. The others could not because they became unconscious before they came to know anything.

There are a few organizations working in the world who prepare persons to communicate information about the spiritual world after death. For example, in London, Sir Oliver Lodge, who was a member of a spiritualist society, tried for a long time after his death to give a message, but failed. For twenty years, in spite of great efforts, no message could be communicated. Some other souls, in fact, informed that Oliver Lodge was trying sincerely to give a message, but tuning in could not be established.

For twenty years, he knocked at the doors of people to whom he had promised to give a message immediately after death. He was prepared by the society for this work. It appeared as if he had tried to awaken his friends from sleep. They would awaken and sit up alert, feeling that Oliver was somewhere nearby, but no one could become attuned in order to receive what Oliver had to say.

Oliver died ready to communicate and continued his efforts for twenty years, but there was no one ready to understand the language of the dead. Very often, some friend passing on the road felt Oliver's hand on his shoulder, knowing full well the touch of his hand. But when he would try to talk to them, the awareness of his presence would become lost. All of his friends would be very much upset over this, but in spite of Oliver's best repeated efforts no message could reach.

Preparations have to be twofold. If someone is capable of telepathic experiences while he is living, if he has developed the capacity to convey thought without words, if he has a capacity to see far off things with closed eyes, then such a person would know many things about the spiritual world.

Knowing is not only dependent on our physical existence. For example, a botanist, a poet, a shopkeeper and a child may go to a garden. They all go to the same garden, but they do not go after the same thing. The child will run after the colorful bees, the shopkeeper would think about his shop problems, the poet would stop at flowers and become lost in composing a poem, and the botanist would try to verify many things about trees.

The shopkeeper can see neither the flowers nor any poem in them. The botanist sees every root, every leaf, every flower, with such analytical eyes that he confirms the knowledge he has gathered over the last twenty or fifty years. None of the others can see what he can see. Similarly, those who die without knowing anything except the body cannot have any recognition of the other world, nor can they establish any relationship with it. They die in a coma, in a deep unconscious state, awaiting a new birth. But those who made preparations in advance will be able to do something. There are scriptures for such preparations.

If, before death, one dies in a scientific way with full preparation for it, with a plan and a methodology as to what he would do after death, then he can do something. There are chances for great experiences. But when a person dies ordinarily, he may take birth immediately or after some years. Then he will not know anything about the condition of the intervening period between births. That is why there is no possibility of direct communication.

> For some time I have been feeling that You are in a hurry. What is that hurry and why? I am not able to understand. But the fact that You are in a hurry is evident from the letters which You have written to some of Your devotees.
> The question also arises whether the purpose for which You had to take birth has been fulfilled. If You have completed the task, then would You explain a statement You once made that You would roam about from village to village creating challenges for people, and if by chance You met with eyes that could become the lamp, You would work on such persons in an all-out effort. You have also said that You would do this so that at Your time of death You will not have to say that You searched for a hundred persons but You could not get them.

I AM in a hurry for three reasons: first, no matter how much time one has, one will always find it insufficient. Always, any amount of time and energy would be insufficient – because the work is as big as the sea, and the energy and the time one has are like the hollow of one's palm. Even if one is a Buddha or a Mahavira, a Krishna or a Christ, the effort cannot be greater than the hollow of the palm, and the expanse of the work is as vast as the sea.

This is only ordinary haste, which is usual. But there is haste for another reason too. Some time periods move slowly so that the time appears not to be moving at all. As we look to our historical past, we will find that time used to move very slowly. Then there are some eras that move fast, in which everything seems to be moving at a high speed. Today we are in such a fast-moving era. Everything is moving at a high speed, and nothing seems to remain steady or stable. If religion continues to move at its ancient slow speed, it will lag behind and die.

In the old days, even science moved slowly. For ten thousand years the bullock cart remained the same. The bullock cart remained a bullock cart and the blacksmith used the same old tools. Everything moved as slowly as a river moving on non-sloping plains. You would not know at all that anything was moving. Banks of such rivers still remain here and there.

In such times, religion also moved slowly. There was a sort of harmony in that movement, and science and religion both were in step with each other. But now religion moves slowly while science and other things are moving at a faster pace. Given these conditions, if religion lags behind and walks hesitantly, then it is no wonder people are not able to keep in step with it. For this reason also there is hurry.

Looking at the speed at which the world's knowledge about matter is increasing and the speed at which science is making great strides, religion should actually remain somewhat ahead of science and achieve a higher speed – because whenever religion lags behind science it causes great harm. Religion should remain a little ahead to guide, because an ideal must always remain a little ahead; otherwise the ideal becomes meaningless. The ideal should always be ahead of achievement and should remain beyond it. This is the fundamental difference between these two.

If we look back at the era of Ram, religion was always ahead of him. If we look to the modern era, man is always ahead of religion. Nowadays only that person can become religious who is very backward. There is a reason for this: it is only because such a person alone is able to keep in step with religion. Today, the more progressive a person is, the farther he is from religion, or else his relationship with religion will remain only formal – will be just for show. So religion must remain in the forefront.

If we look back to the time of Buddha or Mahavira, it will be very surprising to know that those who had the best minds in their times were religious. But in our civilization, if we look to the modern religious man, he has a lesser intelligence. In those days, those who were the leaders, those who had reached the top, were religious people. And now, those who are rustic, rural and backward are religious. The more intelligent minds of our times are not religious. This means that religion is not able to march ahead of man. For that reason also I am in a hurry.

Another reason for being in a hurry is that these are times of emergency, of crisis. For example, when you are going to a hospital, your footsteps have a faster pace than when you are going to your shop. The speed you use to go to a hospital is that of an emergency or a crisis. Today, the state of things is almost such that if some religion is not able to create and put forth a strong vigorous movement it is possible that the entire humanity may be annihilated.

It is a time of emergency, like that of being admitted to a hospital. It is possible that the patient may die before reaching the hospital or before any medicine can be administered or by the time the disease is diagnosed, but the ill effects of this prevalent condition are not affecting any religious thinkers. Instead, they are affecting the younger generations of the entire world, and they have hit the younger generations of the developed nations the hardest.

If American parents tell a son to study for ten years in a university so that he may get a good job, the son retorts by asking whether there is a guarantee that he will live for ten years. The parents do not have the answer. In America, there is little trust in tomorrow. Tomorrow cannot be trusted; it is not certain whether there will even be a tomorrow. Therefore, there is a desire to enjoy today as much and as fast as one can.

This is not accidental. It is like a patient who is lying on his deathbed and may die any moment. The whole humanity is becoming like that. There is a hurry, because if the diagnosis is slow there can be no quick remedy. Therefore, I am in a hurry that whatever is to be done should be done fast.

About my statement that I will move from town to town: I have by now, in one sense, already done that work. I have in mind some people; now it is a matter of working on them. But the difficulty is that it would be better if instead of my keeping them in mind they keep me in mind. And as long as I do not come into their minds, nothing can be done.

But I have started this work also. My going and coming or my staying are all for the purpose of doing something. After preparing some persons, I want to send them out in two years to various towns. They will go. Not one hundred but ten thousand persons will be prepared. These times of crisis are as full of potential as they are of dangers. If time is properly utilized, great potentialities are developed; otherwise the result is calamity.

Many persons can be prepared. This is a time for enterprise, and many people can be prepared for a jump into the unknown. It will happen. I have told you about the outer state of things. But whenever an era of destruction appears near, there will be many a soul that will have reached the last stages of development on the inner plane. Such souls only need a push, and with just that they will take the jump.

Ordinarily, when death is felt to be coming nearer, it can be seen that one begins thinking about what is beyond death. Every individual begins to become religious in such a situation where death is drawing nearer to him. The questioning about what is beyond begins at the approach of death. Otherwise, one's life remains so much engaged that such a questioning does not arise. When a whole era approaches a near-death condition, then millions of people begin to think inwardly about what is beyond. This situation can also be utilized; it has great potentialities.

Therefore, I will slowly confine myself to a room: I will stop coming and going. Now I will work on those who are in my mind.

I will prepare them and send them out. The moving from place to place, which I cannot do myself, I will be able to do by sending out ten thousand people.

For me, religion is also a scientific process, so I have in my mind a complete scientific technique for it. As people become ready, the scientific technique will be passed on to them. With the help of that technique, they will work upon thousands of people. My presence is not needed for that. I was required only to find such people who could carry out that purpose. Now I shall be able to give work to them.

It was necessary to evolve certain principles; that has been done by me. The work of the scientist is over. Now the work is for the technicians. A scientist completes the work, like Edison harnessing electricity and inventing an electric lamp. Thereafter, it is the work of the electrician to fix the bulb. There is no difficulty in that.

Now I have an almost complete picture of the work to be done. Now, after giving people the concept and getting them to do the technique, I will send them out as soon as they become ready. All this is in my mind, but the potentialities are not seen by all. Most people see only the actualities. Seeing the potentialities is a different task, but I can see them.

The conditions that were existing in one small area of Bihar during the time of Mahavira and Buddha can come about very smoothly within the next few years on a global scale. But an absolutely new type of religious person will have to be prepared, a new type of sannyasin will have to be born, a new type of yoga and meditation system will have to be devised. All this is ready in my mind.

As I come across people they will be given these things, and they will further pass along the same to others. There is a grave risk, however, because if the opportunity is lost it will cause great harm. The opportunity must be utilized because such a valuable time as exists today can hardly come again. From every angle, the era is at its climax or peak. Hereafter, there will only be anticlimax. Now America will not be able to progress further; it will only undergo disintegration. The civilization has touched its peak, and now it will disintegrate. These are the last years.

We have noted that India disintegrated after Mahavira and Buddha. After them, that golden crest could not be touched again. People ordinarily think that this happened due to Mahavira and Buddha, but in fact the case is just the opposite. Actually, just before disintegration begins, people of the caliber of Mahavira and Buddha are able to work, not before that — because just before disintegration, everything is in disorder and just on the point of crumbling.

Just as death faces an individual, so now death shows its dark face before the collective consciousness of an entire civilization. And that civilization's collective mind becomes ready to go deep into the realms of religion and the unknown. That is why it was possible that in a small place like Bihar fifty thousand sannyasins could move along with Mahavira.

This can repeat itself again; there is a complete possibility for it. I have a complete plan and a blueprint in my mind for this. In one sense, my work of finding the people I wanted is nearabout complete. Also, they do not know that I have found them. Now I have to give work to them by preparing them and sending them out to spread the message.

As long as it was my work, I knew what I had to do and I was doing it with comparative ease. But now I have to give work to others; now I cannot remain in that ease. I have to hurry up. This is another reason for my hurry. I therefore want to make it clear to all friends that I am in a hurry, so they should also hurry up. If they keep on at the speed with which they are walking, they will not reach anywhere. If they see me in a hurry, then perhaps they will also pick up speed; otherwise not.

Jesus had to do this. Jesus said to the people that the world was very soon coming to an end. But people were so foolish that it was very difficult for them to understand. Jesus said that before their very eyes everything would be destroyed, that it was time for them to make a choice, and that those who did not change then would never get a chance to do so later. Those who heard and understood him became transformed, but most of the people went on asking when that hour would strike.

Now, after two thousand years, some Christian scholars, priests and theologians sit back and think that it seems as if Jesus had made some mistake – because up until now that day of judgment has not arrived: Jesus had said that the event of world destruction would happen before their very eyes – while he was there – that the day of reckoning would come and that those who missed would miss forever. But that time has not come yet.

Was this the mistake of Jesus or have we misunderstood him? Some say that he made such a great mistake because he did not know anything about the matter, and therefore there may have been many other things about which Jesus did not know. Still others say that there is something wrong in our interpretation of the scriptures. But none of these people know that there are deep reasons and a calculated purpose behind what people like Jesus say. By saying these things, Jesus created an atmosphere of emergency in which many people became transformed.

People become transformed only during emergencies. If one knows that one can transform tomorrow or even the day after, he will not do anything today; he will postpone it for tomorrow or the day after. But if he knows that there is no tomorrow, then that capacity for transformation comes into being.

In a way, when civilizations are on the verge of disintegration tomorrow becomes uncertain. One is not sure of the next day. Then the today has to be so compact that it can complete all that has to be done. If one has to enjoy, he has to do it today. If he has to surrender and renounce, that too he has to do today. Even if one has to destroy the ego or transform, that also must be done today.

So in Europe and America, a positive, decisive mentality has come into being that whatever one wants to do must be done today: "Forget the worries of tomorrow. If you want to drink, drink; if you want to enjoy, enjoy; if you want to steal, steal. Whatever you want to do, do it today." On the material plane, this has happened.

I want this to happen also on the spiritual plane. This can run parallel to what is happening on the material plane. I am in a great hurry for this idea to dawn. It is definite that this idea will come from the East. Only Eastern winds could carry it to the West, and the West will jump into it with full vigor.

There are particular places suitable for the rise and growth of certain things. All types of trees cannot grow in all countries. There are particular roots, a particular kind of land, a particular climate and particular water required for the growth of certain things. Similarly, all types of ideas also cannot arise everywhere, because different roots, land, climate and water are necessary for these as well.

Science could not develop in the East. For that tree there are no roots in the East. Religion could develop in the East because for that the East has deep roots. The climate, the land and the water – everything required for its growth – are available in the East. If science has come to the East, it is only from the West. If religion goes to the West, it will be only from the East.

Sometimes there is an exception to this. For example, Japan, a country of the East, can challenge any country of the West in science. But it is interesting to note that Japan only imitates; it cannot be original. But it imitates in such a way that even the original looks pale before it. But still, it is imitation. Japan does not invent anything. If Japan makes a radio, it can outwit America in doing so, but it has to copy the basic one. Japan will be very skillful in copying, but the seed will come from Western countries. It will sow the seed and bring up the plant carefully, but it will never have original seeds of its own.

With religion also, America can outshine and surpass the East. Once the seed of religion reaches there, America will outdo the East in its growth. But all the same, this will be imitation. The initiative, the first step in this matter, lies in the hands of the East.

That is why I am in a great hurry in planning to prepare people in the East who could be sent to the West. The spark will catch like wildfire in the West, but it has to come from the East.

5

THE BIRTH
OF A NEW MAN

March, 1971

What was that event that made You turn toward the spiritual? What was that miracle?

THERE has been no such event. It happens many times that some event occurs and a person takes a turn in life. It also happens that as a result of the collective effect of many events, a person's life is changed. In my life there has been no such event that can be singled out as having caused such a change. However, there have been many events whose collective impact may have caused a turning point, but when this happened cannot be determined. Furthermore, I do not think I ever "turned to the spiritual." I was already in that direction. I do not remember any day when I have not been thinking about the spiritual. From my very first memories, I have been thinking about it.

Many events have occurred in which the collective effect is to be considered. I remember no single event that is so outstanding. Ordinarily, just one excuse sometimes diverts the mind suddenly. However, I believe that the mind diverted toward something by a single event can revert back also. But if the turning is the collective result of many events, then there is no reverting back because that turning is deeper and has entered into the many layers of one's personality. Just as by a single push you can be forced in a certain direction, so also can another push in the opposite direction cause you to return back.

Again, turning by only a single push is a type of reaction. It is possible, but you are not fully ready for it and you simply become diverted. When the effect of that push vanishes, you can return back. But if every moment of life slowly and steadily brings you to a state where even you yourself are not able to decide how you came there, then returning back out of reaction is not possible – because then that condition becomes even part of your breathing, so to speak.

However, one memory in my life which is worth remembering is that of death. It is difficult to tell what I might have thought on that day. My early childhood passed at the house of my maternal grandparents and I had great love for them. I did not stay with my mother and father in my childhood but with my maternal grandparents.

My mother was their only child. They were feeling very lonely, so they wanted to bring me up. Therefore, up to seven years of age, I stayed with them. I had taken them as my mother and father. They were very rich and had all possible conveniences. Therefore, I was brought up like a prince. I came in touch with my father and mother only after the death of my maternal grandparents. Their passing away and the manner in which it happened became the first valuable memory for me because I had loved only them and received love only from them. Their passing away was very strange. The village in which they were staying was about thirty-two miles away from any town. Neither was there any doctor nor any *vaidya,* one who practices ayurvedic medicine.

In the very first attack of death upon my grandfather, he lost his speech. For twenty-four hours we waited in that village for something to happen. However, there was no improvement. I remember a struggle on his part in an attempt to say something, but he could not speak. He wanted to tell something, but could not tell it. Therefore, we had to take him toward the town in a bullock cart. Slowly, one after the other, his senses were giving way. He did not die all at once, but slowly and painfully. First his speech stopped, then his hearing. Then he closed his eyes as well. In the bullock cart,

I was watching everything closely, and there was a long distance of thirty-two miles to travel.

Whatsoever was happening seemed beyond my understanding then. This was the first death witnessed by me, and I did not even understand that he was dying. But slowly all his senses were giving way and he became unconscious. While we were still near the town, he was already half dead. His breathing still continued, but everything else was lost. After that he did not resume consciousness, but for three days he continued breathing. He died unconsciously.

This slow losing of his senses and his final dying became very deeply engraved in my memory. It was he with whom I had my deepest relationship. For me, he was the only love object, and because of his death, perhaps, I have not been able to feel attached to anyone else so much. Since then, I have been alone.

The facticity of aloneness took hold of me from the age of seven years on. Aloneness became my nature. His death freed me forever from all relationships. His death became for me the death of all attachments. Thereafter, I could not establish a bond of relationship with anyone. Whenever my relationship with anyone would begin to become intimate, that death stared at me. Therefore, with whomsoever I experienced some attachment, I felt that if not today, tomorrow that person could also die.

Once a person becomes clearly aware of the certainty of death, then the possibility of attachment is lessened in the same proportion. In other words, our attachments are based on the forgetfulness of the fact of death. With whomsoever we love, we continue to believe that death is not unavoidable. That is why we speak of love as immortal. It is our tendency to believe that whomsoever we love will not die.

But for me love invariably became associated with death. This meant that I was not able to love without being aware of death. There can be friendship, there can be compassion, but no infatuation over anything could catch me. Very deeply did death touch me – and so intensely that the more I thought of it, the more and more clear did it become to me each day.

Thus, the madness of life did not affect me. Death stared at me before the thrust into life began. This event can be considered as the first which left a deep impact and influence on my mind. From that day onwards, every day, every moment, the awareness of life invariably became associated with the awareness of death. From then onwards, to be or not to be had the same value for me. At that tender age, loneliness seized me.

Sooner or later in life – in old age – loneliness seizes everyone. But it seized me before I knew what company meant. I may live with everyone, but whether I am in a crowd or a society, with a friend or an intimate, I am still alone. Nothing touches me; I remain untouched.

As that first feeling of loneliness became deeper and deeper, something new began to happen in life. At first that loneliness had made me only unhappy, but slowly it began changing into happiness – because it is a rule that when we become attached to anyone or anything, in one way or the other we turn from facing ourselves. Actually, the desire for attachment to someone or something is a device for escaping from one's own self. And as the other goes on becoming more and more important to us, to the very same extent he becomes the center for us and we become the periphery.

We continue to remain other-centered for the whole life. Then one's own self can never become the center. For me, the possibility of anyone else becoming my center was destroyed in the very first steps of my life. The first center that was formed broke down, and there was no other way but to revert back to my own self. I was, so to speak, thrown back to my own self. Slowly, that made me more and more happy. Afterwards I came to feel that this close observation of death at a tender age became a blessing in disguise for me. If such a death had occurred at a later age, perhaps I would have found other substitutes for my grandfather.

So the more unripe and innocent the mind is, the more difficult it becomes to replace a love object. The more clever, skillful, cunning and calculative the mind becomes, the more easy it becomes to replace or substitute another for the one lost. The more quickly you replace, the sooner you become free from the unhappiness derived from the first. But it was not possible for me to find a substitute on that very day when death occurred.

Children are not able to find a substitute easily. The place of the love object that is lost remains empty. The older you are the faster you can fill the emptiness, because then one can think. A gap in thought can be filled up quickly, but emotional emptiness cannot be quickly filled. A thought can persuade one faster, but the heart cannot persuade. And at a tender age when one is not capable of thinking but is capable only of feeling, the difficulty is greater.

Therefore, the other could not become important to me in the sense that it could save me from my own self. So I had to live with my own self only. At first this seemed to give me unhappiness, but slowly it began giving me the experience of happiness. Thereafter, I did not suffer any unhappiness.

The cause of unhappiness lies in our attaching ourselves to the other, in expectation from the other, in the hope of gaining happiness from the other. You never actually gain happiness, but the hope is always sustained. And whenever that hope gives way, frustration begins.

Thus, in the very first experience, I became so badly disappointed from the other that I did not try again. That direction was closed for me, and so thereafter I never became unhappy. Then a new type of happiness began to be experienced which can never come from the other. Happiness can never come from the other; what is created is only a hope for future happiness. Actually, only the shadow of happiness is received.

Exactly the reverse is the situation when encountering oneself for the first time. When encountering oneself, unhappiness is experienced in the beginning, but authentic happiness progressively comes about as the encounter continues. On the contrary, encountering the other gives happiness in the beginning, but unhappiness is the end.

So, to me, being thrown upon oneself begins the journey toward the spiritual. How we become thrown back in this way is another matter. Life gives many opportunities for being thrown back to oneself. But the more clever we are, the quicker we are in rescuing ourselves from such an opportunity. At such moments we move out from ourselves.

If my wife dies, I am immediately in search, and then I marry another. If my friend is lost, I begin to search for another. I cannot leave any gap. By filling that gap, the opportunity I would have had to revert back to my own self is lost in a moment, along with its immense possibilities.

If I had become interested in the other, I would have lost the opportunity to journey toward the self. I became a sort of a stranger to others. Generally, it is at this tender age that we become related with the other, when we are admitted into society. That is the age when we are initiated, so to speak, by the society which wants to absorb us. But I have never been initiated into society. It just could not happen. Whenever I entered into the society, I entered as an individual and I remained aloof and separate like an island.

I do not remember that I ever cultivated any friendship, though there were many who wanted to be my friends. Many persons made friends with me, and they enjoyed making friendship with me because it was not possible to make me an enemy. But I do not recall that I have ever gone of my own accord to anyone in order to make any friend. If someone threw himself on me, it was a different matter. It is not that I never welcomed friendship. If someone made a friend of me, I wholeheartedly welcomed it. But even then I could not become a friend in the ordinary sense. I have always remained aloof.

In short, even while studying in school, I remained aloof. Neither with any of my teachers, nor with any fellow student, nor with any other, could I develop such a relationship as would drown me or break my being an island. Friends came and also stayed with me. I met many people as well; I had many friends. But from my side there was nothing that could make me dependent upon them or which would cause me to remember them.

It is very interesting to note that I do not remember anyone.

It has never happened that I would sit pondering over someone with the feeling that if I would meet him it would be very pleasant. If someone does meet me, it makes me very happy, but I do not become unhappy due to not meeting someone. For the state of ultimate joy, I believe that only my grandfather's death was responsible. That death threw me back to myself permanently. I have not been able to revert back from the center. Due to this condition of being an outsider, a stranger, I have seen a new dimension of experience. It is a condition in which, although I am amidst everything, I continue to remain outside.

I became a universe unto myself. This new experience – and a strange one at that – gave me a sort of pain, although it was a joyous pain. It was like this: that at that young age I began to feel and experience a sort of maturity and elderliness. In this experience there was no ego involvement, but an individuality was still there, and that placed me in some embarrassing situations.

For example, I could not accept anyone as my teacher though I was always ready to be a student. But I did not find anyone whom I could call my master. Everyone I found was very much involved in and with life. No one who had not seen death could ever become my teacher. I wanted to respect, but I could not. I could respect rivers, mountains and even stones, but not human beings. This was a very embarrassing situation, and it put me in great difficulties.

I met no such teacher whom I could spontaneously respect, because I never felt that there was anything which anyone knew which was such an absolute truth that without it life could have no meaning. Many times I have felt that various teachers were saying and doing things which looked childish – which even I, at that age, would not say or do. Therefore, I had never felt that I was a small child and that I should remain under someone's protection and guidance. Not that I did not go to anyone: I did go to many people, but I always returned empty-handed and felt that all which was imparted I also knew. There was nothing which could be learned from them.

Therefore, a difficulty arose in that many a time others felt that I was egoistic. It was natural for them to feel that way because I was not able to respect and honor anyone or to obey anyone's command. Everyone felt that I was an immodest and seditious rebel. Up to a particular age, to my teachers, to my elders and to everybody, I have been a discourteous, rebellious, seditious and egoistic person, and they had no hope that I would ever be of any use to anyone in life.

In whatsoever they had put simple faith I could not put any faith at all, and that which they never doubted, I always doubted. To whatsoever they had always stood with head bowed down in *pranam,* I could not even join my hands. I never felt to do so. I never tried to deceive myself, nor did I learn any hypocrisy. If I had no trust, it was so: I could not help it, I did not try to show off anything which I did not believe to be true.

Therefore, this created some difficulties, but it also had its advantages. I was thrown back upon myself from another direction as well, because I never believed or felt that the truth could be learned from others. There was only one way to learn – to learn from myself only. I therefore never knew anyone to be my guru. I was my guru and my disciple as well. If I could not follow anyone blindly, the only alternative left was to search in my own way. There was no one to show me a way that I might follow. I had to walk by myself.

The most valuable result of this was that I had to pave my own way, follow my own discretion, and in every matter make my own decisions. There was no question of taking anyone's help. This being thrown back again and again upon myself proved very valuable.

This does not mean that I distrusted everyone or that I showed any contempt or disrespect to anyone. I simply could not respect anyone, and the natural result of all this was that my doubts became stronger and stronger. I doubted everything.

This attitude also became useful when I began to read and write. Whether I studied the Gita, the Koran, the Bible, or whether I studied Buddha or Mahavira, that doubting instinct was always with me. It never happened that I would keep Krishna a little above the other gods and kill all my doubts. Doubt always remained with me. Therefore, no fanaticism, no blindness, no following or devotion to only one particular religion could result.

The ultimate result of all this was that I remained without any conclusions, full of questions and more questions and doubts. There was no final answer about anything. Whatever answers were there belonged to others, and I could not trust anyone else's answers. Others' answers did only one thing for me, and that was to give birth to ten more questions. No one else's answers could become mine.

So from the very first this condition was dangerous, because to live without any aim was very insecure. I was not even sure of what was just one inch ahead, because that I could come to know only from others. About the path up to where one has traveled one can know positively, but about what lies ahead on the path one has not traveled, one can only know from others. Therefore, for me there was no clear path. It was all darkness. Every next step for me was in darkness – aimless and ambiguous.

My condition was full of tension, insecurity and danger. All my relatives and intimates thought that I was a rebellious and seditious person because of this condition. Slowly people began thinking that I might become mad, such was the situation.

In every small matter there was doubt and nothing but doubt. Only questions and questions remained without any answer. In one respect I was as good as mad. I myself was afraid that anytime I might become mad. I was not able to sleep at night.

Throughout the night and the day, questions and questions hovered around me. There was no answer to any question. I was in a deep sea, so to speak, without any boat or bank anywhere. Whatever boats had been there I had myself sunk or denied. There were many boats and many sailors, but I had myself refused to step into anyone else's boat. I felt that it was better to drown by oneself rather than to step into someone else's boat. If this was where life was to lead me, to drowning myself, then I felt that this drowning should also be accepted.

My condition was one of utter darkness. It was as if I had fallen into a deep dark well. In those days I had many times dreamed that I was falling and falling and going deeper into a bottomless well. And many times I awakened from a dream full of perspiration, sweating profusely, because the falling was endless without any ground or place anywhere to rest my feet.

Except for darkness and falling, nothing else remained, but slowly I accepted even that condition. Many times I felt that I might have agreed with someone, I might have held on to something, I might have accepted some answer. But this did not suit my nature. I was never able to accept anyone else's thoughts.

Inevitably, it so happened that there was no longer any place within me for any thoughts. Now I realize that all answers are nothing but thoughts. If there are only questions, then a person can become thoughtless.

A conclusion is a thought. If there is no conclusion, then automatically a vacuum is created. I did not know this at the time, but a sort of emptiness, a void, came about of its own accord. Many questions circled around and around. But because there was no answer, they dropped down from exhaustion, so to speak, and died. I did not get the answers, but the questions were destroyed.

One day a questionless condition came about. It is not that I received the answers – no. Rather, all the questions just fell away and a great void was created. This was an explosive situation. Living in that condition was as good as dying. And then the person died who had been asking questions. After that experience of void, I asked no questions. All matters on which questions could be asked became non-existent. Previously, there was only asking and asking. Thereafter, nothing like questioning remained.

Now I have neither any questions nor any answers. If someone raises a question, that answer which comes from my inner void is the answer. I cannot say that the answer is mine because I never have any prior thought about it. The answer is not ready in advance. I too hear the answer for the first time when my listener is hearing it. Just as he is hearing it for the first time, I am also. It is not that I am the speaker and he is the listener, nor is it that I am the giver and he is the taker. The answer has come, and both of us are listeners and takers.

Therefore, if my answer is different tomorrow from what it was today, I am not responsible for it because I had not given the answer at all. The same void from which it has come is responsible for changing it. I am helpless. Therefore, you will find that I am very inconsistent. I can be consistent only if "I" am answering. If there is any inconsistency, it is due to that void within me. I have no knowledge of it. Whatever answer comes is not given by me. Since that experience, neither have I asked any question, nor have I sought any answer. In that explosion, the old man of yesteryear died. This new man is absolutely new.

You have asked me if there was any turning point. There was no turning point, but there was death. What is meant by this is that the man who was walking on the path has not taken any turn. Rather, he is dead and is no more. What is, is a new man altogether. Therefore, the question of returning back does not arise. There is no one who has taken any turn. Were that the case, then there would be a possibility of returning back also. But that old man is not there. For example, at a hundred degrees centigrade water changes into steam. Water does not remain as water; it is something else, something new.

Now I do not think from my side. If someone asks something, just as you have done, then I speak. I do not even think; I just speak directly. As far as memory goes, there also I do not think that it is mine. It seems that it belongs to someone else. What I mean is that those things about which I am telling you which happened in the period before the explosion are not mine; they even appear to belong to someone else. It is just as if they were simply heard by me or read in some novel or seen in some drama or somewhere.

Here, so many people request me to write my autobiography. It is very difficult because the one about whom I would write is not me. Whatever I am now has no story. There is no story after that explosion; there are no events after it. All events are before the explosion. After the explosion there is only void. Whatever was before is not me or mine.

When a person writes about himself, it is an autobiography; when a person writes about someone else, it is a biography. If I write a biography, it will not be mine. It cannot be an autobiography because the "I" is no more there. It can be a biography of a person whom I once knew, but who now is no more. It can be about a person whom I once used to be, but who has now ceased to be. Also, it would be like writing about someone whom I have known or heard about, whom I used to see, but who is now dead.

I never knew that these events which took place constituted a search for the spiritual. I came to know only later that what came about was "spiritual knowledge." But the truth is that those who had known me from my childhood would never have believed that I and religion could ever go together. It was beyond their expectations because what they were calling or knowing as religion I had always fought against.

What they were calling worship was just so much nonsense for me. What they called a sannyasin was for me nothing but an escapist. What they called scriptures, to which they used to bow their heads in worship, were but ordinary books for me upon which I could rest my foot. Whatsoever they asserted as being beyond doubt, I dragged into uncertainty and suspicion. Their God, their soul and their salvation were all matters of joke and fun for me.

Their seriousness appeared to me as childish. When I would see them sitting with folded hands before their God, I would laugh and disturb them. All this appeared to me so childish that they could never imagine that I, of all persons, could ever become religious.

If those who had known me during those days prior to the explosion and who have since died should come alive again, and should those with whom I have long been out of touch see me today, they would not be able to even recognize my present self, nor would they be able to imagine that I can be that same person whom they had known.

They could never believe it, because whatsoever they believed as religion I believed to be anything but religion. In their minds, I was an atheist, and a total one at that. To my family members, my friends, my relatives and my associates, I was a great atheist. Therefore, those who suddenly meet me today, after a lapse of about twenty or twenty-five years, will have the shock of their lives. It has happened that those who had become atheists in my company, or because of me, are embarrassed because they have all remained atheists.

Recently I went to a village where I met a man who had become an atheist because of me. He is still an atheist, and he became very frightened. He said that what I had told him then, he had continued to believe as true even until now. So I had no idea that what I was doing then would ever lead me into enlightenment.

According to me one cannot go into it by knowing it in advance. It is something which is unknown. How can one know its address? It is not at any particular place so that by knowing its address one can reach it. One who fixes the address will be a non-religious person. How can one do it without knowing it? Whatsoever a non-religious mind will do will also be non-religious. Therefore, one cannot make it a goal, nor can one reach it knowingly.

Yes, it may happen that someone living in an irreligious way may just become tired of it, and his irreligiousness might break down. Then religiousness will not come, but his non-religiousness will simply break. His non-religiousness will shatter and disappear completely. And one day he may suddenly find that he has become naked. The clothes of irreligiousness will have dropped away and to his surprise he will exclaim, "Aha! This is something new! What has happened is a religious experience!"

Thus, religious experience is a happening, something that is an unplanned occurrence, not an achievement, not a preplanned, progressively attained accomplishment. No one can reach there step by step as if it were on a ladder. But from living – and living irreligiously – that irreligiousness may simply shatter. I say that supreme knowledge cannot be a goal, but the ignorance and false knowledge can disintegrate. And the moment ignorance disintegrates, the remainder – what remains – is supreme knowledge.

About everything my view is similar. No violent person can become non-violent. How can a violent person become non-violent? Whatsoever he does will be violent. In the attempt to be non-violent, he will become violent. He *is* violent, and if he poses as non-violent, he will remain totally violent within. He will use violence to become non-violent.

But what *is* possible is that one day a person can become tired of violence. One who is full of tension – grief-stricken and distressed from his suffering – may be so full of unbearable unhappiness that he will take a jump from violence. It is like suddenly jumping when seeing a deadly snake crossing one's path or like running out of the house that has caught fire. One may become so violent, violence itself can generate so much pain and suffering, that one can reach a point where he can never become violent again. Something within may break and shatter, and one may find that now he has become non-violent.

Thus, becoming non-violent is a happening, not a process or a progressive achievement to where one may climb step by step. Who will climb? That violent person? He will climb only with his violence; he cannot reach non-violence. No matter how many steps a thief might take, the steps will be only those of a thief: they cannot lead him to non-stealing. No matter how many steps a liar may take, they will only be those of a liar: he can never reach any truth. But if the lie totally drops, then there where such a person may find himself will be truth.

So that which is significant in life, supreme, cannot be achieved by our efforts. I therefore did not know what had happened until it happened, and even then I also did not understand it to be a religious happening. How could I understand? Recognition and understanding are always of what is known before. When you came, I recognized you as Tandonji, but I could do so only because I had known you yesterday. If I had not known you before, and if we had met for the first time, ours would be an acquaintance, not a recognition.

Therefore, I could not recognize that happening when it

exploded upon me. The only thing felt was that something new had happened which was not known before. What was felt was this, that what had been there now was no more and what had now happened was not there previously.

It took time to become acquainted. It was an acquaintance known only by asking, "Who are you and what are you?" This acquaintance again was very strange, inasmuch as it was only with myself. Nothing had come to me from outside that I could recognize. Rather, something had dropped from me. That which remained was unknown, and I had to become acquainted with that. Even then this acquaintance is never complete, because daily it takes on a newness. By the time we know it, it becomes still more new. This is the infinite journey of the knowledge of the self. It is endless, beginningless and infinite.

Religiousness is not a dead end, but a supreme end. It is like a river which is flowing: daily the scenery on the banks changes; daily the alignment of trees changes. New rocks and hills come by, and a new moon and new stars are seen. Whatsoever we have known yesterday is lost today. In this supreme experience, one can never say that "I have reached," that "I have realized," that "I have completely known what was to be known." If someone talks in that language, he has not reached at all. One only enters into that experience. He does not reach the end, because it is endless. If someone enters into the sea, he can say that he has entered, that the coast is lost, but he can never say that he has met the sea – because a new coast is never found, and everywhere, all around, there is the sea.

So a religious person cannot write the message about his reaching and his achievement. He can only say that the old is not there and that which is now happening is changing every moment, every day. As such, it is new and again new. It is not possible to say what it will be like tomorrow, because whatsoever it was yesterday is not today. Whatsoever is there today is slowly disintegrating. This unbounded living which renews itself every moment, which never becomes stale, is the religious experience. And we can never make efforts to attain it, nor can we ever fully attain it.

So whosoever says that he has attained it could never have attained it. But he who says that he goes on attaining it more and more daily, but is never able to fully attain it, or who says that when he attains it fully he will tell, or who says that the whole still remains unattained, is the only one who has really attained. Truth is such that something always remains to be known, and yet one feels that it was always known. Our language, therefore, expresses everything wrongly. Those who go through life with an aim – and many do so – never reach.

Recently, someone came and asked me if he could become a sannyasin. I told him, "As long as you feel like asking, do not become a sannyasin, because then one thing is certain: that sannyas is not spontaneous. Sannyas is not to be taken; it cannot be taken. One day it will come to you. Then suddenly you will realize that you are a sannyasin and that you are no more what you were." Then he told me that many people are "taking" sannyas.

To me, whatsoever can be taken at will is false. Religiousness that can be worn is false; religiousness that one tries to achieve is false. Life, death, hatred, violence, unhappiness, pain and anxiety – all these are not taken by us: they have come. Let us live them totally, and from experience, from that living totally, the transcendence will begin.

The more fully we live, the more we find that we are going further and beyond. It is something like this: a person is drowning in a river. If he tries to save himself, perhaps he will be drowned. If he is sinking, then let him sink fully. If he does not try at all to swim, then after reaching the bottom he will find that he has begun to come back upwards. He who is ready to drown will be saved, and he who is afraid of drowning and who struggles will surely drown. The dead float on the water, and the living sink down. The skill of the dead body lies in the fact that it does not do anything, and that keeps it on the surface of the water.

So I came above water like a dead body. I did not do anything for it, nor was I aware of where I was going. Neither do I know today where I am going, nor is there any question as to where I am going. Now, wheresoever I go is the goal and where I reach is just where I had to reach. Now there is no aim. Now there is nothing to be achieved. Now there is no search. But all this did not come about due to any turning. That is, I have never taken a turn, nor is there any event which can be described as one that has brought on the explosion. Many events collectively helped – and then it happened.

In this world, religion has become a great falsehood, because people say that it can be adopted. Whatsoever can be adopted cannot be greater than us. After all, it is the "I" who will be adopting it, is it not? And if "I" adopt it, how can it be greater than me or more infinite than me? When it comes, *we* are not there to grasp it. It comes only when *we* are lost. No matter what we may call it – call it truth, or God, or enlightenment – at such moments of void, it simply descends.

Whosoever has received it has felt that it is God's grace. The reason for saying so is that it did not come by his own efforts. It is not that it is received *only* because of his grace, but it appears so since there is no effort on our part.

That is why I have begun saying that we cannot search for it. How can we search for a God whose name and address we do not know, whom we cannot recognize because he was not hitherto known? How will we be able to search for him? If we know him and recognize him, then there is no need for search. Therefore, I cannot search for him. But if while searching the "I" dissolves, then *he* will find *me*. He knows me well enough.

Perhaps I have been already found by him even now, but I am such a person who is running and running but am still not tired. Even now I am not tired, but he will wait until I drop down totally exhausted. And there where I shall drop is his lap.

6

LIFE IS FULL
OF MYSTERIES

1973

*You have explained to us about the three 'gunas,'
the three basic forces of life, of 'tamas,'
the cause of inactivity, inertia and indolence,
'rajas,' the cause of activity or passion,
and 'sattva,' the cause of serenity,
calmness and knowledge. You have also explained
to us that they existed in equal measure
in the personalities of Lao Tzu,
Jesus, Mahavira and Krishna.
In this connection, it is remembered that You were
a great revolutionary in the past.
In the social, economic, political and religious spheres
You had created much excitement and controversy
throughout the country.
From this it appeared that You were, like Jesus,
activity-oriented or predominantly activity conscious.
But of late, since the end of 1970,
You have been slowly withdrawing Yourself,
and we have a feeling that You have
now become the epitome of serenity.
Is it possible to have such a transformation?*

LET us take certain things into consideration in order to understand this. Firstly, Buddha, Mahavira, Mohammed and Jesus used only one of the three *gunas* as a medium of their expression. *Rajas* was the predominant medium of expression for Jesus and Mohammed. *Tamas* was the predominant quality of Lao Tzu and Raman Maharshi. But Krishna made use of all the three qualities simultaneously as his medium for expression.

There is one more possibility, and I have been making use of it in my own experiments. All the three qualities have been used by me not simultaneously, but one after the other. In my opinion this is the most scientific way of doing it, and that is why I have chosen this way.

All the three gunas are present in all individuals. Because of the mixture of these three gunas in everyone, body and mind take a particular formation. Just as a triangle cannot be made without the use of three lines, there can be no personality without the presence of these three gunas. Even if one of three gunas is missing, the personality will disintegrate.

No matter how predominant the *sattvic* trait may be in a person, the other two will also have to be there, though they may remain hidden or dormant. The other two qualities will have to be present, and their shadow will continuously fall on the predominant sattvic guna. What is meant is that the other two qualities are secondary or subordinate. Even when one quality is predominant, the other two qualities still have to be there.

Krishna has used all the three gunas simultaneously, and they are present in him like the three proportionate lines of an equilateral triangle. Just as the equilateral triangle has three lines of equal length, in the personality of Krishna all the three gunas are present and united in equal measure. Because of this it became very difficult to understand Krishna.

It is very easy to understand a person with one predominant quality. In such a person the other two qualities are dormant, and the personality of such a person shows consistency. But you cannot find in the personality of Krishna the consistency which you can find in the personality of Lao Tzu. The underlying note which is in one word of Lao Tzu is similar to that which is in all his words. In the statements of Buddha also there is close consistency. Buddha said, "Just as the taste of sea water is salty everywhere, in the same way, from wheresoever you analyze my teachings, you will find the same consistent quality."

Jesus and Mohammed have only one predominant quality also. But in Krishna you can find multidimensional qualities manifested. The three gunas at least are positively there, but as hundreds of intermixtures are possible among these three gunas, a variety of new intermixtures of them are manifested in Krishna. That is why Krishna has a multidimensional personality. No person can love Krishna as a whole. One will have to be selective. One will tend to exaggerate and emphasize whatsoever one likes in Krishna, and whatsoever is not liked will be deleted. Therefore, up to now all the definitions of Krishna have been made by people who have been selective. Neither Shankara nor Ramanuja nor Nimbarka nor Vallabhacharya nor Tilak nor Gandhi nor Aurobindo have accepted Krishna as a whole. They have cut out those parts of Krishna's life which have appeared inconsistent and contradictory to them.

For example, Gandhi, who attaches a great value to non-violence, would find it difficult to explain Krishna when he is encouraging and inciting Arjuna to violence. Also, Gandhi considers truth as supreme while Krishna is even capable of telling a lie. This is beyond the understanding of Gandhi. Gandhi will never accept that a person like Krishna can deceive. If Krishna can do this, then Krishna will no longer remain worthy of worship for Gandhi.

There is only one way out of this embarrassment, and that is to explain somehow that Krishna has not really done such things. It is only a story, just symbolic. The battle of the Mahabharata was never actually fought according to Gandhi. For him, the Kauravas and Pandavas are not really human enemies who are battling, but they are only symbolic of the eternal fight between virtue and vice. The Mahabharata is only a story – a parable for him. Gandhi is not afraid of fighting a vice, but he is afraid of hitting a villain. Vice alone can be cut and destroyed for him.

But if it was only a question of destroying or killing vice, Arjuna too would have had no problem. But Arjuna had to kill wicked villainous people. The question of whether it was right for him to kill or not arose only because the people who had arrayed themselves against Arjuna were his own relatives and elders. He had a feeling of attachment and "my-ness" in relation to them, and it seemed to him that the world would have been incomplete, absurd and unenjoyable for him without them.

Krishna's personality is bound to be inconsistent, because all the three gunas are existing simultaneously in him. In me also there will be inconsistency, but not so much as is in Krishna. There is another possibility which I have utilized in my own experiments. All three gunas are present in every individual, and a personality can be complete and total only when all three are utilized. None of the gunas need be suppressed. Neither is Krishna in favor of suppression nor am I in favor of suppression. Whatsoever is there in an individual must be utilized creatively.

In my own experiments I chose to express one guna at a time – only one in a single time period. First I chose tamas, because this principle is in the basic foundation of everyone. When a child is growing in the mother's womb for nine months, it is living in this guna. The child is in total darkness; there is no activity. It is the most inactive state possible. Even the act of breathing has not to be done by the child. It is done by the mother. Nor does the child have to eat; that is also done by the mother. Even the circulation of blood in the body of the child is dependent on the circulation of blood in the mother. The child does not do anything on its own. It is in a condition of total inactivity. There is a child and there is a life, but this life is not having any activity. During that period in the mother's womb there is total inactivity.

Psychologists have concluded that the desire and search for liberation, heaven or salvation is due to an unconscious memory of the experience of the inactive state of life in the mother's womb. The child has known supreme silence in the womb. This memory is hidden deep down in the unconscious. That nine-months' experience in the mother's womb was very blissful, because then there was nothing to be done. There was no responsibility, no burden, no anxiety, no work. There was only existence for you – just being. This state is very similar to the state we call liberation. This experience is hidden within you. That is why, after birth, you are not able to be happy anywhere, and you find that everything is lacking something. Psychologists say further that this can only be possible if you have had a prior experience of blissfulness with which you can compare your present.

Every human being says that life is unhappy. If you have not had any experience of happiness, how could you recognize unhappiness? Everyone is saying that he is in search of happiness. What is this happiness which we are in search of? How can you search after that which you have not previously tasted? How can you desire something which has not been previously known? In the unconscious mind, there is a ray of experience, there is a seed hidden. You have known some bliss, some heaven that was lived, some music that was heard. No matter how much you may have forgotten it, its unquenched thirst pervades your entire existence. Knowledge of its existence lies hidden within. Only for that are we in search.

Psychologists say that the search for liberation is really a search for a cosmic womb, and until such time when the whole existence becomes your womb, the search will continue unabated. This is a very meaningful and valuable statement. But in this connection, it is good to remember first that the child is in a state of inactivity in the mother's womb. During that period there is no question of being active. There is just a blissful silence. The child is in deep inactivity, just sleeping twenty-four hours a day. This is a long sleep of nine months. But just after the child is born, it sleeps for twenty-two hours, then for twenty hours, then eighteen, and slowly it awakens. Years will pass after which the child will stabilize at a sleeping period of about eight hours, and many births will pass until that sleeping period drops to zero – until he will be so totally awake that even during sleep he will be fully aware.

Krishna has said that everyone sleeps except the awakened

one. Before achieving this awakened state, a long chain of births will have to be passed through.

Inactivity is the foundation and blissful silence is the peak. This house which we call life is built on the foundation of inactivity. The middle structure is the active part and the dome of that temple is ultimate bliss. To me, this is the structure of life. That is why I have practiced inactivity in the first part of my life.

The first years of my life were spent, like Lao Tzu, in experiencing the mysteries of the tamas guna. My attachment with Lao Tzu is, therefore, fundamental. I was inactive in everything; inactivity was the achievement sought by me. As far as possible, nothing was done — only as much as was unavoidable or compulsory. I did not so much as move a hand or a foot without a reason.

In my house, the situation was such that my mother sitting before me would say, "Nobody else can be found and I want to send someone to fetch vegetables from the market." I would hear this as I sat idly in front of her. I knew that even if the house was on fire, she would say to me, "No one else can be found and our house is on fire. Who will extinguish it?" But silently, the only thing I did was to watch my inactivity as a witness, in full awareness. Let me narrate some incidents to illustrate this point.

In the last year of my university education, there was one professor of philosophy. Like most professors of philosophy, he was obstinate and eccentric. He was obstinate in his determination not to see any woman. Unfortunately we were only two students in his class: one was myself and the other was a young girl. Therefore, this professor had to teach us while keeping his eyes closed.

This was a very lucky thing for me, because while he would give a lecture I would sleep in the class. Because there was a young girl in the class he could not open his eyes. However, the professor was very pleased with me, because he thought that I also believed in the principle of not looking at women, and that in the whole university there was at least one other person who did not see women. Therefore, many times when he met me alone he told me that I was the only person who could understand him.

But one day this image of me was erased. The professor had one other habit. He did not believe in a one-hour period for his lectures. Therefore, he was always given the last period by the university. He would say, "It is in my hands when to begin a lecture, but it is not in my hands to end it." Therefore, his lecture might end in sixty minutes or eighty or even ninety minutes; it made no difference to him. He would say that he would not necessarily cease to speak when the bell indicating the end of a period rang. Only when the subject begun was completed would he cease to speak. Therefore, during these eighty to ninety minutes I used to sleep in his class.

There was an understanding between that young girl and myself that she would wake me up when the period was almost at an end. One day, however, she had been called by someone for some urgent work during the middle of the period, and she went away. I kept on sleeping and the professor went on lecturing. When the period was over and he opened his eyes, he found me sleeping. He woke me up and asked why I was sleeping. I said to him, "Now that you have found me sleeping, I would like to tell you that I have been sleeping daily, that I have no quarrel with young women and that it is very pleasurable to sleep while you are lecturing."

Sleeping was more or less a sort of meditation for me. I slept as long as I could. It is interesting to note that if you sleep in excess of your requirements, you remain awake and aware even during sleep. If you sleep less than your requirements, then during sleep you become unconscious. You cannot sleep more than your requirements. If you still persist in sleeping after the body's requirements for rest are over, someone inside you remains aware and becomes a witness of all that is happening around you. If you remain lying down for thirty-six hours at a stretch, you will have an inkling of what Krishna means when he says that at night the sage remains awake. If you continue to keep the body in a condition of sleep even after it does not need any sleep, then within you a sort of wakeful sound begins to become audible.

In those days of continuous sleeping, I began to realize that it is possible to remain awake in sleep. I slept during the night, morning and afternoon continually. Whenever there was a chance to sleep I did not miss it. My family members and friends believed that I was totally lazy and that I would not be able to do anything in life. In a way, from their point of view, they were right – but not so from my side. I had made inactivity an experiment in meditation.

There was another professor of mine. He was also a good friend, and he was as inactive as I was. Since he was also living alone, as was I, he suggested that it would be better if we roomed together. I told him that there might be some difficulty in this. Quite possibly, I thought, I might disturb his sleep or he might disturb mine. However, if he still wished that we stay together, it would be necessary to make some arrangements, since both of us were lazy. Even now he is like that. He has not given up this particular quality of his. But he has never made this quality an experiment in meditation; otherwise he would have been beyond it by now.

Bear in mind that within a few days you will be able to transcend anything which you make a part of your meditation. Meditation means transcendence. Anything which you fully and totally enjoy you will be able to transcend. If you experience inactivity fully, you will suddenly find that the inactivity has left you forever. So if there is anything from which you want to be freed, enjoy it fully. For this reason I thought it best to totally enjoy my inactivity first.

When my professor friend and I started staying together, on the very first day I had to settle what would be our arrangements. Until now we had been living apart, so there had been no need for any particular arrangements. First of all he proposed that whosoever got up earlier should go and bring milk. I immediately agreed. I was pleased and he was also pleased. But both of us were in illusion. I had been thinking that there was no need for me to get up first in the morning, but to my dismay he was also thinking the same. About nine o'clock the next morning, I opened my eyes. When I saw him sleeping, I slept again. He awoke by ten in the morning and saw me sleeping. He also wanted to sleep, but there was one difficulty for him. He had to go to the university at eleven o'clock. After all, he was in service, but I was only a student. Thus, I had neither any compulsion nor necessity to go. As it was, I never did attend college regularly.

Ultimately, out of sheer necessity, he had to get up and fetch the milk. By the time he came back I had also got up and would be sitting. He told me that this type of friendship would not work, because now it had become a daily problem. He said he had to go to the university, so he could at best sleep only up to ten o'clock while I could wait for the whole day. It meant that he would have to fetch the milk every day, and if that were the case the friendship could not continue.

I had made it my first principle to refrain from doing anything. For the two years that I was in the university hostel, I never cleaned or swept my room. I kept my cot right at the entrance of my room so that from the door I could jump straight into my cot and from the cot I could jump straight out of the room. "Why should the whole room be unnecessarily crossed?" I felt. Neither did I want to enter into the room, nor was there any question of cleaning it. There was, however, a sort of joy in this.

Things were left the same way that they had been arranged prior to my living there; no change was made. No more was ever done than the minimum that was necessary. Because changing things around required that something be done, things were kept as they were. But due to this, some unique experiences began to dawn, as every guna has its own unique experience. No matter how much rubbish collected in my room, it did not disturb me at all. I had learned to live with that just as I would live in a place which is meticulously cleaned.

In the university where I was studying, new buildings were as yet not constructed. It was a newly established university, and military barracks were used as a hostel. Because the barracks were in a deep forest, it was common for snakes to appear. I used to watch those snakes while sleeping in my cot. The snakes came, rested in the room and went away. Neither did they disturb me at any time, nor did I disturb them.

If there is no feeling to do anything about a thing, many things become accepted as natural. If there is no feeling to do anything in life, the degree of discontent suddenly drops. In those days there was no reason for any discontent, because by not doing anything I had no demands, and there was no question of expecting any fruit or result out of doing nothing. When you do not do anything, then whatsoever comes to you satisfies you. Sometime or the other, some friend, out of pity, cleaned the room and I was filled with a feeling of gratitude.

During the eight or ten days when examinations were on, the superintendent of my hostel used to awaken me at seven o'clock in the morning so that I would not remain sleeping while the examinations were on. He would give me a lift in his car and drop me off at the examination hall. Without effort, I used to earn sympathy and compassion from all, because all had understood that I would save myself from doing whatsoever I could.

Many astonishing things were happening. I am telling you these things so that you can realize that life is full of mysteries. My professor would come and tell me before the date of an examination what I should read in order to answer a particular question. I had never gone to ask anyone for anything. Even after the professor indicated the likely questions, he did not trust that I would read the portion he suggested. Therefore, he would look at me with an inquiring gesture in order to know whether I understood what he had said. He would add that the indicated questions would *definitely* be asked, because he was the one who prepared the exams. There was no doubt; those questions would definitely be asked.

I am trying to tell you that if you attempt to snatch and steal from the world, there will be great opposition everywhere. But if you are in a condition of doing nothing, all doors open and things are simply given to you.

In those days I used to go on lying upon the cot, vacantly watching the ceiling above. I came to know after a long time that Meher Baba had meditated in this manner only. I did this without any effort, because while lying down on a cot what else is there to do? If the sleep was over, I would just go on looking at the ceiling without even blinking the eyes. Why even blink the eyes? It is also a type of doing. It is also a part of activity. I just went on lying there. There was nothing to be done. If you remain lying down like that, just looking at the ceiling for an hour or two, you will find that your mind becomes clear like a cloudless sky – just thoughtless. If someone can make inactivity his achievement in life, he can experience thoughtlessness very naturally and easily.

In those days, I neither believed in God nor in the soul. The only reason for not believing was that by believing something would have to be done. For inactivity atheism is very helpful, because if God is, then some work will have to be done for him. But without any belief on my part in God and soul, by my simply lying down silently, the radiance of both God and soul began to be seen. I did not give up inactivity until inactivity left me. Until then, I had decided to continue on like that – just doing nothing.

I have understood that if one can thoroughly live out the principle of inactivity, thereafter the rajas guna will automatically begin to develop from within, because this is a second quality hidden in the second stage of life. After the first stage is completed and transcended, the second stage, of activity, begins. Activity will grow, so to speak, within you. This activity will also be of a unique type. It is not the activity of a politician, anxious and tense, running for election. If inactivity has been made an achievement and goal by you, if inactivity turns out to be the road leading you to thoughtlessness, then activity will not be motivated by desires. Rather, it will be motivated by compassion. This activity I have also lived through fully.

I never had any feeling to erect barriers in front of a natural process. Whatsoever was happening was allowed to happen. If things were always allowed to happen that way, one would transcend beyond one's usual existence, because then one is not the doer. The doing alone is the doer.

When this second phase – that of rajas – began, I kept on traveling throughout the country. As much as I traveled in those ten to fifteen years, no one would travel even in two or three lives. To speak as much as I spoke during those ten to fifteen years would ordinarily require ten to fifteen lives. From morning until night I was on the move, traveling everywhere. With or without any reason, I was creating controversies and making criticisms – because the more the controversies, the quicker the transition through the second phase of activity. I therefore began to criticize Gandhiji, I began to criticize socialism.

Neither did I have any relationship with these subjects, nor was there any attachment to politics. I had no interest whatsoever in these. But when the entire population of the country was absorbed in these tensions, and I had to pass by this same population, there seemed, even if just for fun, a necessity to create controversies. Therefore, during this transition of my second phase of activity, I engineered a number of controversies and enjoyed them.

If these controversies had been created due to tension-filled actions motivated by desire, it would have brought me unhappiness. But as all this was just for the necessity to develop the rajas guna, just for its expression, there was fun and interest in it. These controversies were just like the acting of an actor.

With one Harigirji Maharaj, a famous Vedantic scholar of Punjab, a big controversy was begun on Vedanta. For me it was just a play. For him it was a serious matter; for him it was a question of principle. He became filled with tension.

With the Shankaracharya of Puri also, a big controversy began in Patna. For me it was a play, but for him it was a question of his very profession. He was so much enraged that he had to be rescued from almost falling down from the platform. His whole body was shaking. But I had to allow the quality of activity full play so that it would be transcended. Many friends tried to stop me, but from my side I did not want to stop until the quality of activity dissipated itself and became spent.

Three weeks out of a month I was sitting on trains. One morning I would be in Bombay, the next evening I would be in Calcutta, the next day in Amritsar, and the following day in

Ludhiana or Delhi. The whole country was the field for my operations. Everywhere, therefore, wherever I went, controversies naturally grew in abundance, because if you do something actively a reaction is bound to be there. Action and reaction are born simultaneously.

During the period of inactivity I practically did not speak at all – or I spoke but little. If questioned repeatedly, I would reply briefly. During the period of activity, I went on speaking even if uncalled for and uninvited. I myself went to people just to speak and my language was full of fire. Now people come to me and ask why I am not now speaking in this same fiery language that used to stop one's very heartbeats.

In those days, there was fire in my language. That fire was not mine; it came out of the rajas guna. That was only one method for burning out the fire of the rajas guna. It must burn in full ferocity so that it can turn to ashes quickly. The milder the fire, the longer it takes to burn out. It was, therefore, a process of total burning out for the purpose of a speedier reduction to ashes.

Now that fire is quenched. Now, just as the sun withdraws its rays in the evening, as a fisherman withdraws his fishing net, I am slowly withdrawing. It is not proper to say that "I" will withdraw. The withdrawal will automatically happen, because the third phase – that of the sattva guna – has begun. Therefore, you may be watching my gradual withdrawal from activities. Fifty thousand persons can listen to me in your place, but I am satisfied if only fifty persons listen – and soon I will be pleased even with only five persons.

Therefore, as the rajas guna subsides and the effects of the sattva guna begin to appear, all actions dissolve into silence. In the state of tamas, all actions cease, but that ceasing is like that of one going to sleep. In the sattvic state also all actions dissolve into silence, but that dissolution is into total awareness.

There is a similarity between the principles of inactivity and of serenity in the sense that both will end in silence. However, the form of silence arising out of the principle of inactivity, tamas, will be that of sleep, whereas the form of silence arising from the principle of serenity, sattva, will be that of silent awareness.

I declare this to be the proper process of life: the first phase pass in inactivity, the second in activity, and the third in serenity. And if you can manage to remain detached during all these phases, then you are in meditation. You must be fully aware during these phases that it is not you who is doing, that it is only the gunas that are at play, that you are not the doer, but only the observer – the witness. And during the play of inactivity, the play of activity, or the play of serenity, if you are only a witness, an observer, if that conviction persists, then all the three gunas will just spend themselves, and you will rest in a transcendental existence which is beyond gunas.

One has to reach that fourth stage which is beyond all the three. It is not even proper to call it the fourth, as there is only nothingness there. None of the three gunas exists in it.

Krishna has expressed himself in all the three gunas simultaneously. I have expressed myself in all, one at a time, in separate time periods. Therefore, in my statements also there will be inconsistency. Whatsoever I said or did during the moments of tamas will differ from what I said or did during the moments of rajas. And whatsoever I spoke or did during my moments of rajas will differ in many respects from whatsoever I have been speaking or doing during my moments of sattva.

Therefore, when one sits down to consider all my statements he will have to divide them into three parts. And there will be many contradictions. It has to be so because their expression is through three different mediums. Consistency among the three is impossible. But if one wishes to search for consistency in my personality, he will have to look for it in the fourth stage which is beyond the three gunas. In the first three stages, the only similarity will be that of the witness observing the three gunas.

BOOKS BY OSHO
ENGLISH LANGUAGE EDITIONS

Early Discourses and Writings
A Cup of Tea *Letters to Disciples*
From Sex to Superconsciousness
I Am the Gate
The Long and the Short and the All
The Silent Explosion

Meditation
And Now, and Here (Volumes 1&2)
The Book of the Secrets (Volumes 1–5) *Vigyana Bhairava Tantra*
Dimensions Beyond the Known
In Search of the Miraculous (Volume 1)
Meditation: The Art of Ecstasy
Meditation: The First and Last Freedom
The Orange Book *The Meditation Techniques of Bhagwan Shree Rajneesh*
The Perfect Way
The Psychology of the Esoteric

Buddha and Buddhist Masters
The Book of the Books (Volumes 1–4) *The Dhammapada*
The Diamond Sutra *The Vajrachchedika Prajnaparamita Sutra*
The Discipline of Transcendence (Volumes 1–4) *On the Sutra of 42 Chapters*
The Heart Sutra *The Prajnaparamita Hridayam Sutra*
The Book of Wisdom (Volumes 1&2) *Atisha's Seven Points of Mind Training*

Indian Mystics
The Bauls
The Beloved (Volumes 1&2)

Kabir
The Divine Melody
Ecstasy – The Forgotten Language
The Fish in the Sea is Not Thirsty
The Guest
The Path of Love
The Revolution

Krishna
Krishna: The Man and His Philosophy

Jesus and Christian Mystics
Come Follow Me (Volumes 1–4) *The Sayings of Jesus*
I Say Unto You (Volumes 1&2) *The Sayings of Jesus*
The Mustard Seed *The Gospel of Thomas*
Theologia Mystica *The Treatise of St. Dionysius*

Jewish Mystics
The Art of Dying
The True Sage

Sufism
Just Like That
Mojud, The Man with the Inexplicable Life
  Excerpts from The Wisdom of the Sands
The Perfect Master (Volumes 1&2)
The Secret
Sufis: The People of the Path (Volumes 1&2)
Unio Mystica (Volumes 1&2) *The Hadiqa of Hakim Sanai*
Until You Die
The Wisdom of the Sands (Volumes 1&2)

Tantra
Tantra, Spirituality and Sex *Excerpts from The Book of the Secrets*
Tantra: The Supreme Understanding *Tilopa's Song of Mahamudra*
The Tantra Vision (Volumes 1&2) *The Royal Song of Saraha*

Tao
The Empty Boat *The Stories of Chuang Tzu*
The Secret of Secrets (Volumes 1&2) *The Secret of the Golden Flower*
Tao: The Golden Gate (Volumes 1&2)
Tao: The Pathless Path (Vols. 1&2) *The Stories of Lieh Tzu*
Tao: The Three Treasures (Volumes 1–4) *The Tao Te Ching of Lao Tzu*
When the Shoe Fits *The Stories of Chuang Tzu*

The Upanishads
I Am That *Isa Upanishad*
Philosophia Ultima *Mandukya Upanishad*
The Supreme Doctrine *Kenopanishad*
That Art Thou *Sarvasar Upanishad, Kaivalya Upanishad, Adhyatma Upanishad*
The Ultimate Alchemy (Volumes 1&2) *Atma Pooja Upanishad*
Vedanta: Seven Steps to Samadhi *Akshya Upanishad*

Western Mystics
Guida Spirituale *On the Desiderata*
The Hidden Harmony *The Fragments of Heraclitus*
The Messiah (Volumes 1&2) *Commentaries on Kahlil Gibran's The Prophet*

The New Alchemy: To Turn You On *Mabel Collins' Light on the Path*
Philosophia Perennis (Volumes 1&2) *The Golden Verses of Pythagoras*
Zarathustra: A God That Can Dance
   Commentaries on Friedrich Nietzsche's Thus Spoke Zarathustra
Zarathustra: The Laughing Prophet
   Commentaries on Friedrich Nietzsche's Thus Spoke Zarathustra

Yoga

Yoga: The Alpha and the Omega (Volumes 1–10) *The Yoga Sutras of Patanjali*
Yoga: The Science of the Soul (Volumes 1–3) *Original Title: Yoga:The Alpha and the Omega (Volumes 1–3)*

Zen and Zen Masters
Poona 1974-1981

Ah, This!
Ancient Music in the Pines
And the Flowers Showered
Dang Dang Doko Dang
The First Principle
The Grass Grows By Itself
Hsin Hsin Ming: The Book of Nothing *Discourses on the Faith-Mind of Sosan*
Nirvana: The Last Nightmare
No Water, No Moon
Returning to the Source
Roots and Wings
The Search *The Ten Bulls of Zen*
A Sudden Clash of Thunder
The Sun Rises in the Evening
Take it Easy (Vols 1&2) *Poems of Ikkyu*
This Very Body the Buddha *Hakuin's Song of Meditation*
Walking in Zen, Sitting in Zen
The White Lotus *The Sayings of Bodhidharma*
Zen: The Path of Paradox (Volumes 1–3)
Zen: The Special Transmission

The Mystery School 1986-1989

Bodhidharma The Greatest Zen Master
   Commentaries on the Teachings of the Messenger of Zen from India to China
Christianity, the Deadliest Poison and Zen, the Antidote to All Poisons
Communism and Zen Fire, Zen Wind
God is Dead: Now Zen is the Only Living Truth
The Great Zen Master Ta Hui
   Reflections on the Transformation of an Intellectual to Enlightenment
I Celebrate Myself – God is No Where: Life is Now Here
Kyōzan: A True Man of Zen

No Mind: The Flowers of Eternity
One Seed Makes the Whole Earth Green
The Zen Manifesto
Zen: The Mystery and the Poetry of the Beyond

The World of Zen *A boxed set of 5 volumes, containing:* *
    Live Zen
    This. This. A Thousand Times This.
    Zen: The Quantum Leap from Mind to No-Mind
    Zen: The Solitary Bird, Cuckoo of the Forest
    Zen: The Diamond Thunderbolt

Zen: All the Colors of the Rainbow *A boxed set of 5 volumes, containing:* *
    The Miracle
    Turning In
    The Original Man
    The Language of Existence
    The Buddha: The Emptiness of the Heart

Osho Rajneesh:
  The Present Day Awakened One Speaks on the Ancient Masters of Zen
  A boxed set of 7 volumes, containing: *
    Dōgen, the Zen Master: A Search and a Fulfillment
    Ma Tzu: The Empty Mirror
    Hyakujō: The Everest of Zen, with Bashō's Haikus
    Nansen: The Point of Departure
    Jōshū: The Lion's Roar
    Rinzai: Master of the Irrational
    Isan: No Footprints in the Blue Sky

**Each volume is also available individually*

Responses to Questions
Poona 1974-1981

Be Still and Know
The Goose is Out!
My Way: The Way of the White Clouds
Walk Without Feet, Fly Without Wings and Think Without Mind
The Wild Geese and the Water
Zen: Zest, Zip, Zap and Zing

Rajneeshpuram

From Darkness to Light *Answers to the Seekers of the Path*
From the False to the Truth *Answers to the Seekers of the Path*
The Rajneesh Bible (Volumes 1–4)

The World Tour

Beyond Psychology *Talks in Uruguay*
Light on the Path *Talks in the Himalayas*

The Path of the Mystic *Talks in Uruguay*
Socrates Poisoned Again After 25 Centuries *Talks in Greece*
The Sword and the Lotus *Talks in the Himalayas*
The Transmission of the Lamp *Talks in Uruguay*

The Mystery School 1986-1989
Beyond Enlightenment
The Golden Future
The Great Pilgrimage: From Here to Here
The Hidden Splendor
The Invitation
The New Dawn
The Rajneesh Upanishad
The Razor's Edge
The Rebel
The Rebellious Spirit
Sermons in Stones
YAA-HOO! The Mystic Rose

The Mantra Series:
    Satyam-Shivam-Sundram *Truth-Godliness-Beauty*
    Sat-Chit-Anand *Truth-Consciousness-Bliss*
    Om Mani Padme Hum *The Sound of Silence: The Diamond in the Lotus*
    Hari Om Tat Sat *The Divine Sound: That is the Truth*
    Om Shantih Shantih Shantih *The Soundless Sound: Peace, Peace, Peace*

Personal Glimpses
Books I Have Loved
Glimpses of a Golden Childhood
Notes of a Madman

Interviews with the World Press
The Last Testament (Volume 1)

Compilations
Beyond the Frontiers of the Mind
Bhagwan Shree Rajneesh
  On Basic Human Rights
The Book *An Introduction to the Teachings of Bhagwan Shree Rajneesh*
  Series I from A – H
  Series II from I – Q
  Series III from R – Z
Death: The Greatest Fiction
Gold Nuggets
The Greatest Challenge: The Golden Future
I Teach Religiousness Not Religion
Jesus Crucified Again, This Time in Ronald Reagan's America

Life, Love, Laughter
More Gold Nuggets
More Words from a Man of No Words
The New Man: The Only Hope for the Future
A New Vision of Women's Liberation
Priests and Politicians: The Mafia of the Soul
The Rebel: The Very Salt of the Earth
Sex: Quotations from Bhagwan Shree Rajneesh
Words from a Man of No Words

Photobiographies

Shree Rajneesh: A Man of Many Climates, Seasons and Rainbows
  Through the Eye of the Camera
The Sound of Running Water *Bhagwan Shree Rajneesh and His Work 1974–1978*
This Very Place The Lotus Paradise
  Bhagwan Shree Rajneesh and His Work 1978–1984

Books about Osho

Bhagwan Shree Rajneesh: The Most Dangerous Man Since Jesus Christ
  (by Sue Appleton, LL.B.)
Bhagwan: The Buddha For The Future
  (by Juliet Forman, S.R.N., S.C.M., R.M.N.)
Bhagwan: The Most Godless Yet The Most Godly Man
  (by Dr. George Meredith M.D. M.B.,B.S. M.R.C.P.)
Bhagwan: Twelve Days That Shook The World
  (by Juliet Forman, S.R.N., S.C.M., R.M.N.)
Was Bhagwan Shree Rajneesh Poisoned By Ronald Reagan's America?
  (by Sue Appleton, LL.B.)

OTHER PUBLISHERS
NEW ZEALAND
After Middle Age: A Limitless Sky *(Compilation, (Hazard Press)*

UNITED KINGDOM
The Art of Dying *(Sheldon Press)*
The Book of the Secrets *(Volume 1, Thames & Hudson)*
Dimensions Beyond the Known *(Sheldon Press)*
The Hidden Harmony *(Sheldon Press)*
Meditation: The Art of Ecstasy *(Sheldon Press)*
The Mustard Seed *(Sheldon Press)*
Neither This Nor That *(Sheldon Press)*
No Water, No Moon *(Sheldon Press)*
Roots and Wings *(Routledge & Kegan Paul)*
Straight to Freedom *(Original title: Until You Die, Sheldon Press)*
The Supreme Understanding
  (Original title: Tantra: The Supreme Understanding, Sheldon Press)

The Supreme Doctrine *(Routledge & Kegan Paul)*
Tao: The Three Treasures *(Volume 1, Wildwood House)*

Books about Osho
The Way of the Heart: the Rajneesh Movement *by Judith Thompson and Paul Heelas, Department of Religious Studies, University of Lancaster (Aquarian Press)*

UNITED STATES OF AMERICA
And the Flowers Showered *(De Vorss)*
The Book of the Secrets *(Volumes 1–3, Harper & Row)*
Dimensions Beyond the Known *(Wisdom Garden Books)*
The Grass Grows By Itself *(De Vorss)*
The Great Challenge *(Grove Press)*
Hammer on the Rock *(Grove Press)*
I Am the Gate *(Harper & Row)*
Journey Toward the Heart *(Original title: Until You Die, Harper & Row)*
Meditation: The Art of Ecstasy
   (Original title: Dynamics of Meditation, Harper & Row)
The Mustard Seed *(Harper & Row)*
My Way: The Way of the White Clouds *(Grove Press)*
Nirvana: The Last Nightmare *(Wisdom Garden Books)*
Only One Sky *(Original title: Tantra: The Supreme Understanding, Dutton)*
The Psychology of the Esoteric *(Harper & Row)*
Roots and Wings *(Routledge & Kegan Paul)*
The Supreme Doctrine *(Routledge & Kegan Paul)*
When the Shoe Fits *(De Vorss)*
Words Like Fire *(Original title: Come Follow Me, Volume 1, Harper & Row)*

Books about Osho
The Awakened One: The Life and Work of Bhagwan Shree Rajneesh
   by Vasant Joshi (Harper & Row)
Dying for Enlightenment *by Bernard Gunther (Harper & Row)*
Rajneeshpuram and the Abuse of Power
   by Ted Shay, Ph.D. (Scout Creek Press)
Rajneeshpuram, the Unwelcome Society *by Kirk Braun (Scout Creek Press)*
The Rajneesh Story: The Bhagwan's Garden
   by Dell Murphy (Linwood Press, Oregon)

FOREIGN LANGUAGE EDITIONS
Books by Osho have been translated and published in the following languages:

Chinese	German	Japanese	Punjabi	Tamil
Czech	Greek	Korean	Russian	Telugu
Danish	Gujrati	Marathi	Serbo-Croat	Urdu
Dutch	Hebrew	Nepali	Sindhi	
Finnish	Hindi	Polish	Spanish	
French	Italian	Portuguese	Swedish	

WORLDWIDE DISTRIBUTION CENTERS FOR THE WORKS OF OSHO

EUROPE

Belgium
Osho Indu Distribution
Coebergerstraat 40
2018 Antwerpen
Tel.   03/237 2037
Fax   03/216 9871

Denmark
Osho RISK Bookstore
Boegballevej 3, Toenning
8740 Braedstrup
Tel.   07575/2500

Finland
Unio Mystica Shop
for Meditation, Books, Music
P.O. Box 186
00121 Helsinki 12
Tel.   3580/665 006
Fax   3580/665 811

Italy
News Services Corporation
Via Teulie 14
20136 Milano
Tel.   02/5830 0039
Fax   02/832 3683
Comp. node 39-50

Netherlands
Osho Publikaties Nederland
Vianenstraat 48
1106 DD Amsterdam
Tel.   020/969 372
Fax   020/890 241

Norway
Osho Devananda Meditation Center
P.O. Box 177 Vinderen
0319 Oslo 3
Tel.   02/149 1590

Spain
Distribuciones "El Rebelde"
07192 Estellencs
Mallorca - Baleares
Tel.   071/410 470
Fax   071/719 027

Sweden
Osho Madhur Meditation Center
Fridhemsgatan 41
S - 112 46 Stockholm
Tel.   08/514 270
Fax   08/184 972

Switzerland
Osho Mingus Meditation Center
Asylstrasse 11
8032 Zurich
Tel.   01/252 2012

United Kingdom
Osho Purnima
Centre for Meditation
Spring House, Spring Place
London NW5 3BH
Tel.   01/284 1415
Fax   01/267 1848

West Germany
The Rebel Publishing House GmbH*
Venloer Strasse 5-7
5000 Cologne 1
Tel.   0221/574 0742
Fax   0221/574 0749

AUSTRALIA & NEW ZEALAND
Osho Meditation & Healing Centre
P.O. Box 1097
Fremantle, WA 6160
Tel.   09/430 8864
Fax   09/384 2822 c/o Raymond

Rebel Books Mail Order
P.O. Box 193
Papakura N.Z.
Tel.   09/292 2602

NORTH & SOUTH AMERICA
United States
Chidvilas Inc.
P.O. Box 17550
Boulder, CO 80308
Tel.   303/449 7811
Fax   303/449 7099
Order Dept. 800/777 7743

Osho Viha Meditation Center
P.O. Box 352
Mill Valley, CA 94942
Tel.   415/381 9861

Also available in bookstores nationwide at Walden Books

Brazil
Osho Jyotsana Meditation Center
Rua Capitao Salomao No. 74/201
Rio de Janeiro, RJ CEP 22271
Tel.   021/226 7124

Canada
Publications Rajneesh
P.O. Box 331
Outremont, P.Que. H2V 4N1
Tel.   514/276 2680

ASIA
India
Sadhana Foundation*
17 Koregaon Park
Poona 411 001, MS
Tel.   0212/660 963
Fax   0212/664 181

Japan
Eer Osho Neo-Sannyas Commune
Mimura Building 6-21-34
Kikuna, Kohoku-ku
Yokohama, 222
Tel.   045/434 1981
Fax   045/434 5565

*All books available AT COST PRICE

OSHO MEDITATION CENTERS AND COMMUNES

There are many Osho Meditation Centers throughout the world which can be contacted for information about the teachings of Osho and which have His books available as well as audio and video tapes of His discourses. Centers exist in practically every country.

FOR FURTHER INFORMATION CONTACT

Osho Commune International
17 Koregaon Park, Poona 411 001, India